Motoring on Regional Byways

BORDER COUNTRY

CHRISTOPHER TRENT

Motoring on Regional Byways

BORDER COUNTRY

Byway motoring in Northumberland,
Durham and the Border Country
of Scotland, illustrated with
32 photographs by the author

LONDON

G. T. FOULIS & CO. LTD

1-5 PORTPOOL LANE

E.C.1

First impression March 1968

© *Rupert Crew Ltd. 1968*

SBN 85429 079 6

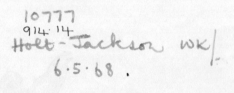

MADE AND PRINTED IN GREAT BRITAIN BY
MORRISON AND GIBB LIMITED, LONDON AND EDINBURGH

CONTENTS

ILLUSTRATIONS

BYWAYS OF THE BORDER COUNTRY

ALL THE TOURS described in this book belong to the Border country in the sense that the places through which they pass are steeped in the history of centuries of intermittent warfare between the English and the Scots and in the thousands of legends which make this part of Britain one of the most romantic and interesting. There is no exact geographical definition of Border country. One might almost say that it depended on the character and historic legacy of the places concerned, and the further one goes from the actual line of demarcation between England and Scotland, the more is this true.

Because of the absence of exact definition people have attempted to define it in various ways. One ingenious way is to assert that everything is Border country where in the Middle Ages every farm and every residence was defended by a pele tower, where even the vicarages were minor stone-built fortresses. It is not only ingenious but in a sense remarkably near the mark, for the pele tower is the hallmark of the farming country liable to be ravaged by armies derived either from Scotland or England riding across the land, looting as they went, and firing every building which they happened upon. The remarkable thing is that in these conditions the medieval farmers of Northumberland and Berwickshire continued to exist—not only that but brought an increasing area of the countryside under cultivation.

The definition implied by the tours in this book is not very far from that simple one but a little wider in scope. On the east coast Berwick-upon-Tweed is, of course, the Border town of all Border towns, one which for centuries changed hands so often that it was difficult to say that it was Scottish or English. Down the coast from Berwick there is a succession of fortresses, full-scale castles as opposed to the farmer's pele, many of which were long held by the Percy family and used sometimes not only to repel the Scots but to defy the King of England.

So we have the Norman-founded castle of Bamburgh, built on the Whin Sill, a basaltic rock which runs right across the narrow neck of England and forms a geological boundary of its own. Bamburgh was certainly a Border fortress and even now, when it has been sadly bedevilled, still looks every inch the part. Equally the great Percy fortress of Alnwick is a Border castle, the vast but now ruined castle of Warkworth and Dunstanburgh standing on its cliff looking out across the North Sea, now only a fragment of what was once a mighty defence.

Though it was not built primarily as a Border fortress, it would be unfair to exclude the Norman Newcastle, which guards the crossing of the Tyne and has given its name to the largest of all Tyneside cities and towns, while the castle palace of the Bishops of Durham on a cliff high above the almost encircling Wear, as impregnable a position as that of any castle in England, was an essential part in the line of protective fortresses.

The Newcastle and the castle palace of Durham, together with some smaller castles commanding the main crossings of the rivers running east-west, such as Bowes Castle and Barnard Castle, bore the brunt of Scottish attacks. If they were overcome or even bypassed, as occasionally happened, there was nothing to prevent Scottish armies bursting forth into the Vale of York and threatening York itself. They were the medieval equivalent of Hadrian's Wall against the Picts, in the sense that once Hadrian's Wall was breached there was little or nothing to stop invading tribes until they reached the broad acres of Yorkshire.

So, logically, the Border country south of the Scottish boundary is assumed in this book to be the modern counties of Northumberland and Durham, together with a small part of Cumberland which links the boundary of Northumberland with the Solway Firth and includes Carlisle, which stood in relation to the western marches almost precisely as Berwick did to the eastern and changed hands almost as many times, though its strong castle by the banks of Eden thwarted many an attempted invasion. In the direction of Scotland's western hills the actual boundary between England and Scotland runs for very many miles across hill country as deserted as any south of the Caledonian Canal. The Cheviot itself is only the highest of a chain of hills with all the appearance of mountains which reach in a long and virtually unbroken line almost as far as the vale of Eden. From the

motorist's point of view their great virtue is that they are crossed
by several roads which reveal much of their grandeur and convey
much of their sense of loneliness, where it is possible to drive
round the Cheviot near enough to its upper slopes to share in the
magnificent vistas which it commands and in the barren country
of moorland and heather-clad slope which compose it.

Northward of the actual Border the coastal strip from Berwick
to St Abb's is clearly Border country, together with the Lammermuir Hills, which form the hinterland of this rocky and inhospitable coastline. For the rest, the Tweed is the effective
northern limit of the Border country, though for the sake of
completeness we have included one tour in the Moorfoot Hills,
which rise from the Tweed's north bank. The real country of
Border legends and warfare lies to the south of it. This is all hill
country to a greater extent than the corresponding landscapes of
Northumberland and Durham, largely a country of heather hills,
broken by a number of lovely green valleys, every one of which
we explore. And so our ways take us not only along the valley of
the Tweed, with its wealth of historic towns and interesting
castles, but along the valley of the Yarrow Water, up Ettrick
and through Teviotdale, as well as into the heart of the Tweedsmuir Hills themselves.

Finally, to the west we have the county of Dumfries, which is
bordered by the Solway Firth and includes many spectacular
viewpoints, as well as a large number of historic towns on the
lower ground. The real distinction between England and
Scotland is less here than in many places. Once you reach
Dumfries, however, you are in the heart of Scotland and look
across the waterway of the Nith to the remote Scottish hinterland
of Galloway where its mountains on a clear day dominate every
scene to the west.

Tyneside motorists are very lucky in commanding within the
scope of a long day's tour nearly two-thirds of the routes outlined in the chapters which follow. The same is true, to a lesser
extent, of motorists from Durham and the big industrial centres
of County Durham, such as Sunderland and Chester le Street and,
of course, Durham City itself. But for the visitor there are
scores of centres with accommodation to suit every purse, not
so much in these towns as in the country to the west, at Hexham
and Corbridge in the valley of the Tyne, at Alnwick and Wooler,

which is at the foot of the Cheviot Hills, or at the small coastal towns of Warkworth, Alnmouth and Bamburgh. Then there is Berwick, a favourite centre commanding almost the whole countryside which we traverse, and the numerous townships in the extreme south of Scotland and the Scott country, in Melrose, for instance, and Kelso and Selkirk, and in the extreme north of the area, in Peebles, or further south in Hawick. In the western areas there is Carlisle and the Scottish towns of Moffat and Dumfries. That is only a small selection. Other good centres are mentioned in the various chapters. One thing is certain—for a country which is seemingly so remote the problem of where to stay is a far less acute one than might be expected.

Nearly 2,500 miles are described in detail in the following pages. The routes will undoubtedly suggest other routes. In a sense you cannot go wrong because once you are away from the industrial centres of Northumberland and Durham you will not find a town which cannot be traversed in a matter of a few minutes, and almost every route which you follow will reveal some worthwhile facet of a countryside which is never for a moment dull, is always rewarding and frequently exciting.

Wherever you go, there are two ways which on no account should be missed, both relatively new ways so far as the motorist is concerned. One is up Ettrick, the other up Coquetdale above Alwinton. Those are two of the finest roads in all the Border country, each ending in the heart of green mountains with all the grandeur and beauty of the Border hills.

CHAPTER TWO

EXCITING WAYS IN THE COUNTY PALATINE

ALL TOO MANY PEOPLE, natives as well as visitors, write off
County Durham as totally unsuited to byway pleasure motoring
except in the western marches where its moorland roads rise
towards the high ridge of the Pennines. In fact lowland Durham
has many scenic highlights as well as a wealth of historic interest
reflected in its many links with the storied past.

First and foremost in its list of historic sites is the City of
Durham and its cathedral 'half House of God, half fortress
'gainst the Scots' as it has been described. Then there are historic
castles still inhabited, like Raby Castle at Staindrop, fragments of
the medieval bishop's palace at Bishop Auckland, as well as
romantic ruins like those of Barnard Castle and Bowes Castle.
Above all, County Durham has at Jarrow in the fragments of
St Paul's Monastery one of the very few links which exist in the
north between modern Christianity and the monasticism of the
seventh century long before the devastating raids of the Norsemen
wiped the Christian religion for a time from the face of the land.

This first tour is suitable for readers from almost any part of
Tyneside, as well as from Sunderland or Durham. It serves as
an introduction to the pleasant byways and rolling countryside
of south Durham. About a hundred miles in all from Newcastle,
it is well within the scope of a single day's motoring, more
especially as the first few miles inevitably are not strictly byways
but take us through South Shields (where there is a ferry link
with Tynemouth) and Sunderland along quickish roads which
are still worth traversing on their own account as well as because
they are the key for motorists coming from the north to the
pleasures of the southern part of the county where after Easington
it is byways all the way. Motorists from Durham may prefer to
join the route at Easington, coming by way of A181 and B1283.

If our start is at Newcastle we cross the river on the Great
North Road, going south to Gateshead and there fork left on the

5

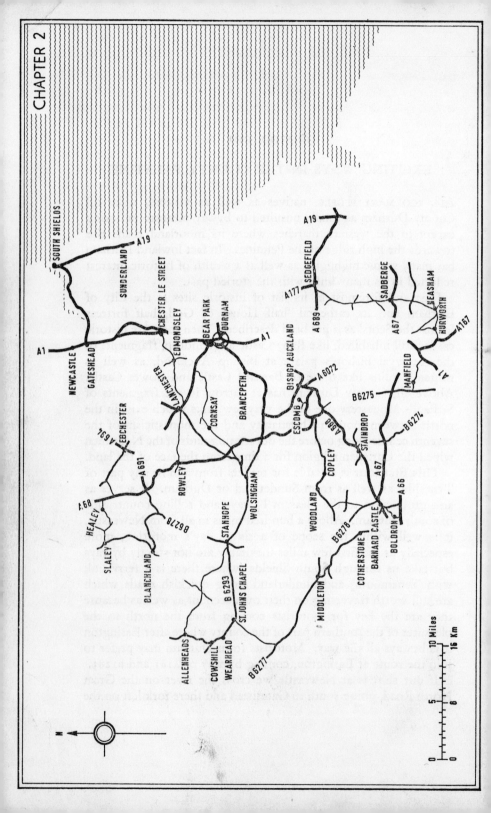

handsome new road which leads quickly and painlessly into Jarrow, which is well signposted at every important turn. There is no need to go into Jarrow centre. Instead we make directly towards South Shields and find the remains of St Paul's Monastery overlooking the square basin, its sides about half a mile long, which forms a natural enlargement of the bed of the Tyne and is known as Jarrow Slake.

The supreme interest of St Paul's is that it was the monastery in which St Bede the Venerable wrote the history on which so much of our knowledge of Anglo-Saxon England is based, especially that part of it which refers to the introduction of Christianity to the Court of Kent by St Augustine and its spread to the north country under the aegis of St Paulinus.

It is probable that St Paul's was founded on or near the site of a Roman station in 682. After its destruction by the Danes it lay waste until it was re-founded as a cell of Durham Cathedral priory in 1075, when a good deal of the original material was re-used. Today the pre-Conquest monastic church is still in use as the chancel of the present parish church, while the fragmentary monastic buildings retain at least one triangular-headed doorway, which is probably as it was built at the end of the seventh century. This is one of the most historic places in England, yet curiously little visited even by the people of Tyneside.

And so following the coast road into South Shields we pass the ferry approach to North Shields, from which we turn left if we are approaching from that direction (i.e. from North Shields or Tynemouth or Whitley Bay). We soon pass the site of a Roman fort, of which unfortunately scarcely anything can be seen though the excellent museum is signposted on our right. Soon we emerge on South Shields' grassy Bents for a most invigorating ride by the sea, where we look for the last time across the estuary of the Tyne to Tynemouth, dominated by its medieval castle. At the end of the promenade and the long stretch of firm golden sands, we continue to A1183 for Sunderland, still over grassy cliffs and never far from the sea, of which we are in view all the way to Marsden Bay, with here and there a distant glimpse of a rocky cove and the detached limestone rocks many of which on a sunny day seem virtually covered in seagulls. Next we pass the Marsden lighthouse and the first of the coastal collieries though this one is not obtrusive and is certainly not in sight long enough to spoil the general impression of beauty which this ride gives.

As we enter the County Borough of Sunderland there is another stretch of fine sands and at the end of the promenade an always interesting view of the harbour, sometimes, when one or two fine ships are in port, a more than ordinarily fascinating one. We follow the road beside the harbour into the town centre, crossing the spectacular metal bridge over the Wear. At least there is no fear of missing the way for the next few miles, for we follow the signposts which show the way along A19 south, usually with the additional information that it leads to Stockton. So we pass the handsome museum building, housing exhibits which are claimed with some reason to be the most interesting in the county. We have a brief sight of some of the modern shops which make Sunderland an up-to-date shopping centre as well as a great commercial and industrial town, but see little else of it: it is our purpose to escape into the country with all possible speed.

Our road, A19, takes us past a charming park, gay with flowerbeds, and through a suburb where the roads are tree-lined, then suddenly we come into the open again with the sea clearly visible on our left. We only turn inland where the Seaham Harbour turn goes straight ahead, continuing on A19 towards Stockton. It is remarkable how green the country looks between here and Easington, considering how close it is to coalmining and industry. Several pleasant transverse valleys break up the scene effectively.

At Easington we cross the crossroads in sight of the church, which has one of the finest of Norman towers in the county, and almost immediately leave the main road for B1283, signposted Durham, continuing to the first crossroads, where at the 'Pemberton Arms' our way is to the left for Sedgefield. This is the most convenient point for Durham motorists to join the tour. We pass the New Shotton colliery village, quite unlike the traditional picture of such villages, trim and pleasant and well built, with the colliery far from the road and generally unseen. Beyond it our way takes us through luxuriant woodlands. On reaching A181 we turn right towards Durham. This, though a main road, is attractive and unspoilt. It only skirts one village before we turn off it after about two miles for Sedgefield on B1278, continuing into Sedgefield village.

The gatehouse, which retains its Norman archway, leading to the castle buildings of Durham. (Chapter 2.)

Looking across Weardale from the road to Stanhope. (Chapter 2.)

The mid-Georgian market cross and town hall of Barnard Castle. (Chapter 2.)

The Saxon church of Escomb, built mainly with stones from the Roman fort of Vinovia. (Chapter 2.)

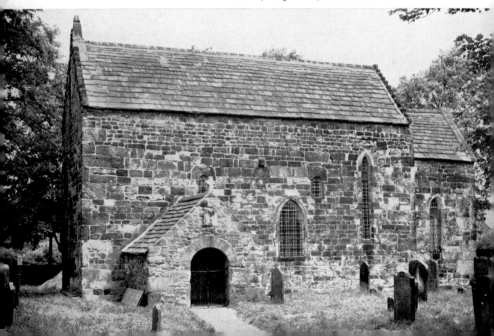

Sedgefield is probably best known for its traditional game of Shrovetide football, a free-for-all on the village green accompanied by many traditional observances and ending in much drinking of beer, but a spectacle well worth seeing if one happens to be in the neighbourhood at the time. Apart from its football fame, Sedgefield is an extremely pleasant place which deserves that often misused word 'pretty'. Wide greens fringe its main street, many of its houses are Georgian, a few rather earlier. One on our right, the finest of them all, is dated 1707. The church is medieval though much restored. Altogether it is a place which demands a pause for a few minutes' exploration.

At the first road junction we go straight on by A689, but in just a quarter of a mile turn left where the signpost reads Darlington past the compact but agreeable steeplechase course which has contributed as much fame to Sedgefield as Shrovetide football! At the next T-junction, where we turn left, our way is still signposted Darlington but this is by no means a main road, rather an attractive byway which leads on to and through rolling farming country, rich and fruitful for an area so far north, with a preponderance of arable fields though the pasture land also looks excellent and there are numerous herds of cows which help to supply the milk for the nearby industrial towns. There can be few parts of England where the market for agricultural produce is so near yet the country so unspoilt and thinly populated.

We leave the Darlington signposts 5 miles short of it, turning left for Sadberge and in the latter village cross A67 for Middleton St George, passing on the village green an exceptionally large boulder which was discovered during excavation for the Stockton and Middlesbrough reservoir, a geological curiosity which seems quaintly out of place on the village green.

It is pleasant enough going for the next 2 miles, though a good deal more level than much of the country we have traversed so far. Beyond the level crossing at the 'Fighting Cocks' inn we go forward in a wider road and after half a mile fork right for Middleton One Row. Just beyond the railway station we bear right for Neasham, so completing a rather complex series of turns, the first on this route which might reasonably give difficulty. Now we are once again in mixed farming country, the level landscapes on our right bounded by the dark line of the Pennines.

At Neasham we reach the banks of the Tees and follow a

lovely reach of the river right-handed beyond the village, continuing to Hurworth and Croft. Of the three, Hurworth is by
far the most attractive, an unselfconscious riverside village built
alongside a long main street with wide green fringes and some
lovely Georgian houses which have been kept in perfect repair.

At Croft we cross the river, bearing left into the North Riding
of Yorkshire on the way to Northallerton but, just beyond the
'Spa' hotel, leave the main road for a turning on the right to
Barton. The country, of course, is little different whether you are
looking at it from the Yorkshire bank or the Durham bank.
The only difference here is that pleasant winding lanes link
together a number of villages on the south bank, whereas on the
north there is only Darlington and a main road which does no
sort of justice to the beauty of the valley.

A quarter of a mile after leaving the main road at Croft we fork
right again for Barton, continuing on this narrow lane over the
green fields to the major road, A1 (from the weight of traffic which
generally uses it one would not suspect that this really is
England's first road). We turn right in it for a quarter of a mile
then left where the signpost shows Cleasby, but at the approach
to this village, another attractive one strung along a green, we
turn squarely left and go through Manfield, 2 miles further along
the valley, where we pass the medieval church with its embattled
tower.

Now we reach the Roman road which once linked some of the
important settlements of the Brigantes and, above all, the
garrison town of York with the outposts of the Roman Wall in
Northumberland by way of Corbridge. We turn right in it,
B6275, signposted Piercebridge, where we cross the Tees again
back into Durham county. The village of Piercebridge, yet
another built round a wide green, is on the site of a Roman camp
which guarded the crossing of the Tees.

At the end of the village we continue on B6275 towards West
Auckland but after 2 miles turn left at a crossroads for Staindrop,
following the signposts to it. The country is still quite typical of
Teesdale but, whereas when we were driving south towards the
Tees the bold outline of the Pennines was on our right and
ahead, here a high ridge forms the backcloth of the scene on our
left. At Staindrop we turn right but it is worth crossing the
bridge on our left to see the village and, above all, the church,

which is architecturally a fine one and has the added interest of
many monuments covering hundreds of years to the lords of
Raby Castle, especially the powerful Nevill family, who included
among their number Warwick the Kingmaker.

Continuing on our way we pass the entrance to Raby Castle,
of which incidentally there is a fine glimpse from the road, but it
is well worth remembering that it is open to the public on certain
days of the week, currently Wednesdays and Saturdays in the
summer and daily in August. This is one of the most interesting
castles in Durham, a fourteenth-century fortress with eighteenth-
and nineteenth-century additions, making it a great palatial
residence, well known for its magnificent collection of pictures.

We continue alongside the park towards Bishop Auckland and
at its end turn left for Cockfield. In just over a quarter mile,
where the Cockfield road turns right, we go straight on for
Butterknowle. Here the country is much more hilly especially
on our left even though we remain within the orbit of cultivated
fields. At the foot of a long hill we bear right, still making for
Butterknowle, on B6282 but very soon leave the Butterknowle
road, continuing on the major road which is signposted Bishop
Auckland. Where this turns right, however, on the slope of a hill
after about a quarter of a mile we go straight on in a minor road,
a very lovely road lined with tall trees at first, then hedged and
green-fringed. Soon we pass the 'Malt Shovel' inn and continue
on this lonely straight road through a scattered hamlet, neglecting
several left turns. On reaching a T-junction we turn right where
the signpost reads Hamsterley, bearing left for it soon afterwards
and right at the next T-junction after crossing a river.

Now we drive on for Bedburn and Wolsingham going straight
on when we reach a major road and straight on again where the
major road turns left. This all sounds rather complicated but
is really much simpler than it sounds. Our way is high above the
lovely wooded valley of the Bedburn beck. Soon we turn left
steeply into the valley where the signpost reads Wolsingham,
crossing the river by a huge derelict mill. Bedburn was once a
thriving commercial community before the industrial revolution
led to the concentration of industry. The mill is all that remains
from those distant days when Bedburn stockings knitted at the
mill had a ready market and spades and other tools were manu-
factured in great number at the nearby forge. It remains a lovely

place in its wooded gorge and the derelict mill adds rather than detracts from its unusual beauty.

We continue uphill, rising to a bracken-covered ridge between two wooded gorges, the only place on this route where we approach a thousand feet above sea-level. We bear left for Wolsingham and there cross the Wear into the village turning right in the main street for Crook, and forking left for Tow Law on a road which is later signposted Lanchester. We keep straight on for Lanchester where the Tow Law road veers off to the right. In another mile, however, we take a right fork (also confusingly signposted Tow Law), crossing A68 at Inkerman, and the next crossroads where our way is once more signposted Lanchester.

This is one of the finest roads in County Durham, with magnificent views over the Browney valley towards the sharply etched outline of the moors. We continue to Lanchester, bearing left downhill at a wider road and crossing the Browney. In Lanchester itself we turn right on B6296 under the railway arch into the village, right on A691, and left beside the church in Peth Bank. Lanchester is a place well worth exploring either on this or on the subsequent tour which also passes through it—probably to better effect on the second occasion when we pass through it early on the tour, rather than now, when our thoughts are probably firmly fixed on return to base.

Peth Bank climbs steeply, as its name suggests. On reaching a crossroads we go forward, crossing a major road near a prominent television mast and at the next T-junction turn right for Chester le Street. It is still green wooded hill country, surprisingly in view of our proximity to industrial Durham. In just over a mile we turn right in a rather obscure turning for Edmondsley (the turn is marked by a telephone box) and at Edmondsley cross a major road for Waldridge. At a T-junction we continue to Chester le Street if we are making for Tyneside or follow the signposts back to Durham. For those who started the tour at Tynemouth or South Shields a useful road, B1288, leaves the Newcastle road on the right about halfway between Chester le Street and Gateshead and links with the main roads to Jarrow and South Shields and there is, of course, a direct road from Chester le Street to Sunderland by A183. Whatever the ending, our thoughts are bound to be with the wonderfully attractive vistas of south

Durham and of the roads we have traversed on the edge of the moorlands from Raby Castle northward.

The tour which has been described shows only part of the beauty and interest which can be found in lowland Durham. **The next tour** goes further afield and in a sense is more conventional, because it takes us into upper Teesdale and Weardale, which many Tyneside motorists make for as a point of honour when the sun is shining. I hope that some of the roads will be new to most readers, including perhaps the one which links Teesdale with Weardale and is one of the several roads which have the right to compete for the title 'highest carriage road in England'. Certainly it exceeds 2,000 ft by a comfortable margin, which means that in all but the finest weather it is above cloud-level. The moral, therefore, seems to be that this is a tour for fine days, a whole day tour of about 110 miles if the start is made at Durham, correspondingly longer from Tyneside, about 130 miles from Newcastle if the start is made by the main road as far as Durham.

Incidentally, Durham is quiet on Sunday mornings and the tour might give an opportunity to spend an hour on the Durham rock to renew acquaintance with the vast Norman cathedral and with the Bishop's Palace and the many attractive houses which line the castle square, a group of buildings unique in England, just as the view from the Wear of the castle and cathedral is one of the finest in the North country. The palace is now part of the University of Durham and its most historic parts are frequently open to the public, though unhappily not on Sundays.

Our way from Durham is by A690, the Crook road, which at one point is signposted Willington, shortly leaving the outskirts of the city as we approach Brancepeth, the first of several surprises on a most exciting route. Brancepeth is an attractive as well as a curious manorial village; one can drive straight up to the church of St Brandon past the castle, which in a sense out-castles all castles. You will see what I mean when you have your first sight of it. It is on the site of an ancient fortress which was greatly admired by Leland, the Elizabethan chronicler. There are records of this castle from the twelfth century onwards and the estate was held early in the seventeenth century by Robert Carr, Earl of Somerset. Little of the ancient castle remains. In fact all that one can see as one drives to the church is modern, the massive gateway, the blind walls, the tiny pierced windows which can give no light, the whole thing a nineteenth-century travesty of medieval life. Yet it is singularly impressive. It comes as no surprise to learn that wounded officers who were nursed here during the first world war likened it to a prison.

The church, too, is worth seeing, if only for its Jacobean oak carving—the chancel screen, the pulpit and the box pews. The wood and stone effigies of the Nevill family, who at one time held Brancepeth as well as Raby, are another distinguished feature.

Continuing through the village and over a short green interval, on reaching the outskirts of Willington we drive left for Newfield into the valley of the Wear, crossing the river, climbing the hillside on the further bank and going straight on over crossroads at its summit, and again at a second minor crossroads. One and a half miles from Willington we turn right away from the threat of Binchester Blocks along a pretty close-hedged lane, now making for Bishop Auckland and closely hugging the banks of the Wear, where there are a number of excellent draw-offs which positively invite the wayfarer to stop for refreshment.

Our first view of Bishop Auckland Castle is on a hill across the meadows, and a very impressive one it is. We climb into the town finding the entrance to the castle and park just to the left of our way on the Durham road. The old castle of the bishops has largely disappeared but the ornate chapel which stands apart from the present bishop's residence was formerly the twelfth-century great hall, while the lodge is an admirable example of seventeenth-century architecture. If you are prepared to take a short walk there is also in the park about 300 yards north-east of the castle a deer shelter which was built in 1760 by Bishop Trevor and is a good example of the Gothic architecture of the time.

We return from the castle to the market place and bear left on the Crook road, A689, then towards the end of the town but before descending a hill leave the Crook road for B6284, the Etherley turn, at a subsequent junction bearing right for Witton Park. Our direct way is along the Witton Park road at the next crossroads but it is well worth turning right for Escomb church, which is well signposted.

Escomb is one of the proudest parts of Durham's heritage, a

Saxon church built from the stones of the Roman fort of Vinovia and little altered through the centuries. It still looks what it is, one of the oldest churches in the kingdom. The keys are kept at a cottage on the green beside it, currently No. 40, but a great deal of interest can be seen without entering it. As the Bishop of Durham has said, the distinction of Escomb is that it has no history. That is one reason why it has survived intact when so many others have been swept away to make room for larger churches. It is probably of seventh-century date, almost as early as the church of the monastery of St Paul at Jarrow. Only the porch and a few windows have been added to the original fabric, which consists of a high nave, long and narrow, and an almost square chancel. The lower parts of the walls are certainly entirely of Roman stones though some stones in the upper parts may be of later origin. A fascinating feature is that one of the stones on the north wall is marked with the inscription LEG VI, i.e. the Sixth Legion, which was at York from the early part of the second century. The assumption is that a detachment of this legion was stationed at Binchester (Vinovia). Another feature of special interest is that the unusually high chancel arch is in all probability a Roman arch brought from Vinovia and re-erected here. The rude stone cross behind the altar is certainly pre-Norman and may indeed be earlier than the church, one of the 'Saxon crosses' which were often erected by Saxon communities after Christianity had been accepted but before a church could be built.

Returning from the church to the Witton Park turn, we continue along the latter quiet road by a course which is as straight as that of the proverbial crow. There are several temptations which must be avoided to turn right or left where the way ahead is a relatively minor road. Later there is no difficulty when our road is signposted Hamsterley. So we pass the entrance to Witton Castle, a comparatively recent addition to the historic homes open to the public. The castle was built in the fifteenth century, though the keep has been modernized and the chief links with the Middle Ages are the defences of the courtyard wall, with its two fine gateways and towers at the angles of the walls. It is open daily from April to October.

We cross a subsequent main road, still following the signposts for Hamsterley but less than a mile from it, just before a bridge, turn left into an obscure unsignposted tree-hung lane, a riot of wild flowers in their season. If this lane is missed the alternative is to go forward into Hamsterley and turn left, but it is not nearly such an attractive way. The lane first rides high above the Linburn beck, then crosses it by a built-up ford and climbs steadily to a height of about 700 ft.

At a T-junction we turn left where there is a long view over the valley of the Linburn beck. This is not yet moorland but it has all the feeling of the moors with its roads and fields bounded by low stone walls. At the next junction we turn right for Bedburn then left in a quarter of a mile for The Grove. Now there is an extensive vista over Hamsterley Forest, which we skirt for nearly three miles and wonder perhaps at what a vast difference afforestation has made to some Durham landscapes, though without rancour for this was virtually unproductive land before the sturdy conifers were planted in its barren soil.

When we emerge once more into open country we take the left fork for Woodland and there turn left in a major road but after 200 yards bear right into a green valley where the signpost reads Bishop Auckland but in Copley fork right for Barnard Castle, rather an easy turn to miss. Soon our view is across the thousands of smiling acres of Teesdale as we descend gradually to pastoral country where hedges begin to take the place of stone walls. We follow the signposts into Barnard Castle, turning right into Galgate and later bearing left on the Bowes road.

The fragments of the medieval castle are on our right here and can be explored but it is only fair to say that we have the best of all views of the castle on our route a little later just before we cross the Tees. We pass the fine market cross which was built in 1747 and is surmounted by an octagonal building which was designed as a town hall. The church is a handsome landmark on the other side of the road, which is the way to the Bowes museum, the vast French-style chateau to which admission is free and which contains a wonderful collection of paintings by the old masters and also china and curiosities derived from every part of the world. It was built and endowed in mid-nineteenth century by John Bowes, a highly successful farmer and racehorse owner who married a French actress known as, even if she could not claim the name of, Countess Montalbo.

We leave Barnard Castle by the Brough road, A67, passing under the castle walls and crossing the river, then turning right on the other side of the bridge and continuing on A67 briefly. At the 'Royal Star' inn, however, we bear left, then right at the next fork by a school where the road divides at a triangle. So we reach the village of Boldron, where we bear first right then left for Bowes and on reaching a major road, the Roman road across the Pennines, turn right as far as Bowes Castle, about two miles along the road.

Our direct way is to turn right at the approach to Bowes on the Barnard Castle road but if we have not done so before it is a must to visit Bowes Castle, to which admission is free and which lies just behind the main street on the left. It is a massive Norman stone keep which was built about 1170 and is almost alone among the Norman castles of the north in that it never formed the nucleus of later palatial buildings but remained a fortress purely and simply, a keypoint in the medieval defences against the Scots. It lies within the Roman fort of Lavatrae and much of the material used in building it is almost certainly taken from the Roman fort. Altogether it is as impressive as it is surprising.

Now we follow the Barnard Castle main road but soon leave it for a left fork signposted Cotherstone, crossing a stretch of heather-covered moorland and at Cotherstone turning left beside the pretty green. Near the end of the village we fork left for Baldersdale, keeping right at two subsequent forks, the first about two miles from Cotherstone and unsignposted, the second signposted Baldersdale North, descending steeply to cross the outflow of a large reservoir. As we climb uphill there are fine retrospective views of the reservoir on our left, looking for all the world like a natural feature of the landscape.

At a T-junction we turn left, still making towards Baldersdale North, and at the next signpost turn right for Grassholme, continuing on this gated road over the high moors more than 1,000 ft above sea-level to the Lune reservoir, which is seen in the distance as soon as we have crossed the highest point. It is a really wonderful view which owes as much to nature as it does to man's contrivance, with the two lakes of Lunedale clearly visible and the moors rising on either side of them to desolate craggy summits.

We cross a crossroads on to a gated road into Lunedale, continuing over the reservoir by a stone bridge, and at the next major road bear right into Middleton. A special feature of interest along this road is provided by the basalt columns in a quarry beside the road. One can see the similarity between this quarry formation and the natural basalt columns of the Giant's Causeway in Northern Ireland. Basalt outcrops like this give the extreme north of England some of its most distinctive scenery, including some of its major waterfalls where the basalt has defied the power of water to wear it away, while surrounding softer rocks have been levelled. It is also the rock of the Whin Sill, which stretches right across the narrow neck of England from Bamburgh Castle to within sight of the Solway Firth.

In Middleton we turn left by the memorial fountain for Alston, continuing along this road, B6277, along one of the prettiest parts of Teesdale, passing High Force, a waterfall well worth seeing, especially after heavy rain. Beyond the scattered village of Langdon Beck we bear right for St John's Chapel, crossing the high boggy moors on which the only things that grow are rank grass and reeds—a stretch of country which is utterly empty of everything except a few hardy sheep and of which the most significant feature is provided by the new black and white fog posts by the roadside. This is the road which competes for the proud title 'highest carriage road in England', reaching an altitude of 2,056 ft. I do not know of one south of the Border which exceeds it in height.

It is a steep descent into Weardale, which we reach at St John's Chapel, a trim village and incidentally a fine classical chapel. There we turn left for Alston and drive on through Ireshopeburn to Wearhead, where we cross the river to Cowshill, beyond which we bear right steeply uphill for Allendale, soon crossing briefly into Northumberland, and at the attractive village of Allenheads turning right for Rookhope.

The climb by conifer woods is a long one before we reach the summit at a cairn and cross once more into County Durham. After that there are immense moorland views as we follow the course of the Rookhope burn, which is marked by a number of disused lead mines, some of them retaining their early nineteenth-century buildings and winding gear, deliberately preserved in one or two cases so that these relatively primitive mining installations unbeautiful though they are may not be forgotten for ever.

At the further end of Rookhope we fork left on a minor road past the chapel on the hillside and drive along a high shelf road which soon commands magnificent views of the Wear valley, ultimately descending to it. We turn left in the valley road into Stanhope, where we go forward for Wolsingham, also signposted Crook. Thereafter we follow roughly the same route as in the previous tour, bearing left for Tow Law and for Lanchester. Later, however, we avoid the main turning to Tow Law and take instead the second minor fork on the right, which although signposted Tow Law runs well to the north of it, and cross A68 at Inkerman for Cornsay.

Now we continue along the ridge road for Cornsay village, drive through it and at the next crossroads turn right for Durham, crossing a subsequent major crossroad for Esh along another high road commanding a breathtaking view of the broad valley on the right. At the 'Board' inn we follow the main road round to the right, over a hill and on to the edge of another smiling valley, continuing to Durham by Bearpark and A1, in which the way is to the right, or for Newcastle to the left.

Just before we leave the country we pass the entrance to Ushaw College, one of the most famous Roman Catholic colleges in the north country, founded in 1804 for the exiled priests and students of the French College of Douay. The buildings, in their magnificent situation on the ridge between the Browney and the Deerness valleys, are conspicuous and magnificently contrived, the more modern parts blending admirably with the work of the early nineteenth century, their chief feature the number of chapels which have been added from time to time, including the elaborate and tasteful chapel of St Cuthbert, which has pride of place in the south front and was dedicated in 1884.

The last tour in this series is a short one of the Pennine moors with its apex at the unique village of Blanchland, perhaps the best introduction to this beautiful district on the borders of Durham and Northumberland that can be devised. The tour is routed from Durham but can equally easily be followed from Newcastle or any of the Tyneside towns.

All routes join at Lanchester, to which the easiest way from Newcastle or Gateshead is by the route described in the previous tour in reverse, or more directly, if less picturesquely, by A692 from Gateshead and A6076, which leaves it at Sunniside and leads fairly directly by Stanley to A691 at the approach to Lanchester.

The way from Durham to Lanchester is country almost all the way. We leave the city by A691 signposted Lanchester, following the Browney valley, one of the best views of which is from Witton Gilbert churchyard. In any case it is worth making the detour to the church by School Lane at the beginning of the village not only for the view but to see the church, which is clearly a late Norman building, though very much restored. Thereafter we continue through the village and after about a mile fork right for Burnhope along a road which rides high above the Browney valley, giving splendid views across it and far beyond. By the television mast at Burnhope we turn left for Lanchester, descending steeply into its huddled group of houses by the river, and turning right at the church, another fine Norman one, also much restored with many later additions. The Norman chancel arch is exceptionally fine, and there is a Roman altar in the porch serving as a link with the Roman fort (Longovicium) at Lanchester (just over a mile away) which stood on the line of Dere Street, the Roman road which led from York to the Wall and eastern Scotland.

At the green we bear left then right for Wolsingham, past the site of this Roman fort (nothing survives above ground). At a five-road junction we bear right for Rowley over a varied landscape, broken up by belts of forestry, and later cross A68 for Healeyfield. After that we continue along the same road, variously signposted Waskerley and Stanhope, soon rising to the moorlands and climbing above the 1,000-ft contour. We pass the high-set 'Moor Cock' inn at Waskerley, just beyond which a signpost shows the way to a reservoir in the midst of the moorlands. At this point it is not possible to see it; however, if we neglect a left turn to Waskerley village we climb to a still higher altitude and have a splendid retrospective view over the reservoir and the heather-clad moors.

At the Edmondbyers turn (the road here exceeds 1,500 ft above sea-level) we go forward on the Stanhope road but in just over half a mile turn squarely right for Blanchland, now rising even higher to above the 1,600-ft contour, with Horseshoe hill (1,703 ft) distinguished by its television mast on our right. On a clear day there is an unobstructed view ahead across the valley

of the Tyne to the Cheviot, whose outline is unmistakable. Far
to the left our view comprehends the whole country of the
Roman Wall and the greater part of Northumberland. Soon we
top the summit and are looking down into the welcoming
Derwent valley, green and fertile, a wonderful contrast with the
moorlands and heather-clad moors we have traversed. We cross
a little stream into Northumberland and reach Blanchland in
another half mile.

It is almost incredible that Blanchland should be not more
than 25 miles from Newcastle in a straight line, so remote is it,
so totally unspoilt. The abbey was a Premonstratensian house
founded in 1165 and dissolved like all the other abbeys in the
reign of King Henry VIII, in this case 1539. Its claim to unique
distinction is that many of the buildings of the village are directly
descended from the monastic buildings. The abbey church, only
a fragment of the original with more recent additions, is the
parish church, its finest features, perhaps, the Norman font and
tower arch, apart from the thirteenth-century cross which is a
conspicuous feature of the churchyard, in which John Wesley
preached before the church was restored. Lord Crewe, the then
Bishop of Durham, made it possible for divine service to be
re-instituted in 1752.

The 'Lord Crewe Arms' was originally the Abbot's house and
guest house. The archway which leads into the square was part
of the massive entrance gate of the convent. The cottages in the
square, or at least those which face south, have been fashioned
out of the monastic refectory, while the remainder were also
originally part of the monastic buildings. In fact there is scarcely
a building in Blanchland which cannot trace its ancestry back to
the days of the White Canons.

We leave Blanchland with regret by the Edmondbyers road,
back into County Durham, following the Derwent valley through
Blanchland Forest, and after nearly two miles take the first
turning on the left for Riding Mill, skirting for some distance
the new reservoir which has so completely changed the appearance of this countryside, immersing the valley of the Derwent
and substituting a wholly artificial landscape with new roads and
a new layout, though one of great beauty. When at last we leave
the reservoir we turn left at a T-junction for Slaley and right at a
subsequent fork for the same village, shortly entering an extensive

and dense conifer plantation. When we emerge into open country
we turn right at a crossroads by a group of cottages, our way
signposted Prudhoe, and follow this road for several miles
through and beside much new forestry, crossing A68 and a
second main road, the Roman road, now B6309.

In the first hamlet we reach we must look out for a narrow
right turning to Hedley just short of the 30 mile speed limit sign
at the beginning of the village. There is another superb view
over the Tyne valley as we climb to over 800 ft, going through
the little hilltop village of Hedley.

Newcastle and Gateshead motorists go forward after Hedley
for Greenside and home. If we are making for Durham, however,
we turn right for Ebchester, dropping down to the Derwent,
with the distant complex of Consett on the skyline.

Ebchester is on the site of the Roman station of Vindomora
and the church stands just within the confines of the fort. Much
of the material from which it was built was taken from the
Roman fort, as was commonplace in such instances, and there is
said to be a Roman altar with an eagle sculptured on it built into
the modern tower. Can you find it? The church incidentally
is dedicated to St Ebba, the first Christian Princess of North-
umbria. Before reaching the church we cross the river and the
main road right-handed (the church is just to the left) for Leadgate.
At the second crossroads by the 'Hat and Feather' inn we bear
left for Medomsley but almost immediately turn right and follow
the ensuing straight road for some miles, crossing all crossroads,
one by the 'Jolly Drovers' right-handed. It is a most pleasant
return to Durham's outskirts, which we re-enter by the Browney
valley road by which we left it. Our last highlight is a fine view
down the valley to Durham cathedral rock, which rises so
abruptly and dramatically above the general level of the land.

CHAPTER THREE

VALLEY OF THE TYNE AND THE ROMAN WALL

THE ROMAN WALL extended from Wallsend-on-Tyne to Bowness on Solway. It was built in A.D. 120 to 126 under the supervision of the Emperor Hadrian and strengthened during the following century. It remains unequivocally Britain's most spectacular link with Roman times. Because it runs through largely uninhabited country it has been possible to excavate and reconstruct the forts, mile castles and turrets along its course, while many archaeological finds of the utmost significance have been brought to light. Fragments of the Wall have been reconstructed well within the boundaries of Newcastle upon Tyne, but the great variety of its historic interest is further west between the crossing of the North Tyne and the moorlands round Greenhead and Gilsland.

One of the tours in this chapter takes the motorist to many of the most important remaining parts of the Wall and will enable the thousands of people who nowadays are interested in Britain's remote past to build up a picture of the northern defences of the Roman province. The other tours in this chapter are chiefly of scenic interest. One takes us out of the valley of the South Tyne to the valleys of two of its most distinguished tributaries, the East Allen and the West Allen, which unite a few miles before joining the Tyne. They are certainly the most distinctive features of the Tyne watershed and the route, though it covers a few well-known roads, is wonderfully attractive. We will take this first in order, though it is not necessarily first in precedence.

The majority will probably come from Newcastle or Gateshead but the tour is an equally suitable one for Durham motorists, the two roads joining at Greenside on a hill above the Tyne and the point where the last of Tyneside's industrial developments are left behind. From Newcastle the way to Greenside is clear and mercifully swift, for there is little of beauty until we have left

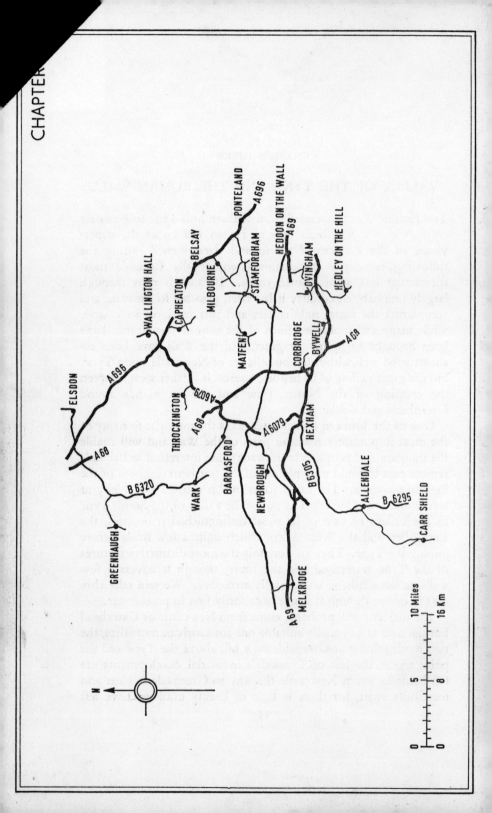

Triangular-headed
Saxon doorway,
St Paul's Monastery,
Jarrow.
(Chapter 2.)

The 'Lord Crewe
Arms', Blanchland,
originally the Abbot's
house and guest house
of the former
Premonstratensian
abbey. (Chapter 2.)

The Browney valley near Lanchester.   (Chapter 2.)

The inner harbour of Sunderland.   (Chapter 2.)

the waterway of the great river. We leave central Newcastle by
A695, crossing the Tyne at Blaydon, continuing through the
latter, and soon afterwards turn left on the signposted road to
Greenside. When we reach Greenside we bear right by the war
memorial for Chopwell. Nothing could be simpler.

If we are starting at Durham we leave by the Great North
Road, A1, but turn aside from it to go through the centre of
Chester le Street, turning left by the church on A693 for Stanley
at the further end of the main street and driving on through
Pelton, still making for Stanley. After about a mile we turn right
on the minor road signposted High Urpeth, where we bear left
at the junction steeply downhill over the river Team and climb
the further hillside on the Sunniside road.

This is a surprisingly pretty road for one so near industrial
places. At the next crossroads soon after a railway bridge we
turn left for Stanley and left at a major road T-junction. Immediately after we have entered the urban district of Stanley we leave
the road by the first turning on the right through what was once
a railway bridge. The road is narrow and rough but it soon
improves, so we must beware of being discouraged. We turn
sharp left by a group of cottages and then after almost a mile of
breezy motoring over the uplands turn right (it is the first
turning on the right) at the end of a wood and the beginning of a
steep descent. Our road to the right keeps high. There is a long
view to the Cheviot before we reach a main road, turn right in it
for about 200 yards, then left on B6310 signposted Shotley
Bridge. Shortly, in Burnopfield's main street, we fork right for
Rowland's Gill into the valley of the Derwent, passing the
entrance to one of the National Trust's most recent properties,
the Gibside Chapel.

A short drive along a good track leads to the chapel car park,
which is beside the mile-long avenue which links the chapel with
the statue of Liberty at the top of a 140-ft-high column. The
chapel is a really lovely example of Georgian architecture
designed by James Paine in the first half of the eighteenth
century. It was commissioned by Sir George Bowes, a notable
country lover, as well as a successful coal owner. Gibside Hall,
a reputedly magnificent Jacobean mansion, is no more but the
chapel is a worthy monument to the Bowes family (who were also
responsible for the Bowes museum) and has been restored to

B.C.—3

virtually its original beauty, a masterpiece of design in the Palladian style.

After crossing the Derwent into Rowland's Gill we turn left on a major road by the 'Towneley Arms', then bear right on B6315 for Greenside. Immediately after passing a small colliery winding gear at the 'Pack Horse' inn we turn sharp left by the war memorial and so join the route from Newcastle. Now the two routes go forward together.

At the next fork we turn right for Hedley along a high road which commands splendid views of the Derwent valley across the chessboard pattern of fields, broken here and there by woodlands. On our right there is a view across the Tyne valley to the Border hills.

At Hedley on the Hill we go straight on for Stocksfield and soon descend steeply to the valley of the Stocksfield burn, turning left at a major T-junction near the foot of the hill and crossing the next major road for Scales Cross and the following one for Slaley. This road continues for about four miles through heavily afforested country. At one point we cross a crossroad for Blanchland and on reaching the main Blanchland-Hexham road we cross it, too, for Whitley Chapel. After the bridge over the Devil's Water (the part of the Devil in carving this valley is not known) we turn right towards Hexham, half a mile short of Whitley Chapel. Soon we cross another little stream, the Ham burn, driving on for Newbiggin and continuing to the first crossroads, which we reach after about a further two miles.

The crossing is unsignposted, insignificant and very difficult to identify but the key to the whole of the next part of the route. We turn left and then go straight on, crossing a major road in half a mile and passing the Hexham steeplechase course before reaching another major road, in which we turn left towards Allendale. This is a perfect byway route and certainly one which is well worth finding. The views all the way are magnificent and varied but mainly across the valley of the Tyne towards the uplands of the Border country. The only alternative way through Hexham is not nearly so attractive.

At the first signposted fork we bear left for Allendale and soon see miles of the valley of the East Allen stretching away from us towards the high moors of the Pennines, the skyline broken here, as in so many parts of the Border country, by the chimneys of long abandoned lead mines. And so to Allendale town, the metropolis of these two dales and nowadays a minor holiday centre, just as in Victorian times it was regarded as a health resort. It is high and breezy and a pleasant looking small town with a fine square and a tree-shaded main street but its real value is as a weekend centre for a most intriguing part of the Pennine moors.

We go forward on the Nenthead road and at the head of the dale fork right for Coalcleugh, and right again in about a quarter of a mile for the same destination over some of the most desolate Pennine country imaginable, yet a landscape with a real distinction of its own. Two miles short of Nenthead we turn right for Hexham.

Here we are only a little below the 2,000-ft contour and it is interesting to see a well-set-up farmhouse sheltering under the crest of the hill and rejoicing in the name of Sunnyside. One hopes it is genuinely the sunny side! Several other farmhouses which we pass as we descend are deserted until we reach the tiny village of Carrshields. However, we soon reach the relatively fertile West Allendale valley bearing left at one point for Nine Banks. Our road closely hugs the river bank until at a junction we bear left for Whitfield and shortly cross the river by an old stone bridge. Half a mile further we join a major road, in which we bear right, the only road which traverses this part of the dale. That is our reason for including it on a byway route. It has many dramatic moments, especially where it crosses the river and climbs into hanging woods, negotiating a very sharp bend, then rides high above the river valley.

At 'Carts Bog' inn we leave the main road, turning sharply right on B6305 for Langley, and just beyond a reservoir go forward over crossroads for Hexham. Now we are driving parallel with the Tyne. At the approach to Hexham we turn right in a major road and left at the war memorial to the magnificent priory church which faces the market house, the ancient prison, and the many old houses which combine to make Hexham one of Northumberland's most pleasant towns. The priory church is on the site of a Saxon church counted as one of the most magnificent in Christendom; its Norman successor which was destroyed during a Scottish raid was almost equally fine. Today it is still a magnificent example of medieval architecture and according to some authorities the richest in Northumberland.

We leave the market square by Hall Stile Bank, crossing the Tyne on the way to Alnwick, but immediately beyond the bridge turn right for Corbridge, now following the north bank of the river. After passing the entrance to the Roman fort of Corstopitum, which we shall visit on our Roman Wall tour, we turn right where the way is signposted Newcastle, and so past Corbridge church on A68. It is, of course, easy to follow this fine highway back into Newcastle but it is far preferable to leave the main road a mile beyond Corbridge at a wood where the signpost reads Styford Hall. So we drop down to the bank of the Tyne, bearing left along it, with many a glimpse of the broad and here unspoilt river.

It is well worth turning aside to Bywell to see the two churches of St Peter and St Andrew, almost side by side, the fine gatehouse of the castle of the Nevill family, and the village cross. One says village, but today there is no village. The communities which once filled its two fine churches have vanished. A special feature of interest of the church of St Andrew is its Saxon tower, one of several in this part of the county.

We return to the through road and continue towards Stocksfield but turn left for Ovington, once more following the river bank for nearly two miles. At the Ovington turn we leave the river, going on for Ovingham, where we return to the river bank, bearing left at Ovingham church, which has a tower similar to that of Bywell's St Andrew. Our way is signposted Wylam, where finally we say farewell to the river after driving along one of its loveliest reaches. From that point Newcastle is well signposted through Heddon on the Wall, less than ten miles to the city centre. The total length of the tour from Newcastle is about 100 miles.

The tour of the Roman Wall is a well-known one, in many ways the most fascinating of all the tours which it is possible to carry out from Newcastle in a single day. Many visitors come from the U.S.A. and from Europe to explore the Wall, and one wonders what proportion of Newcastle people really know it intimately. Yet it is not difficult to know, for most of the main features of interest along the Wall are readily accessible by car or by a short walk from the car. As a Victorian commentator said

'It is not necessary to dismiss one's carriage until one has reached the western part of the Wall round Winshields Crags' and there even today full justice cannot be done to it except on foot.

This brainchild of the Emperor Hadrian was built to make the province of Britain secure against the attacks of the tribes who lived to the north and were completely outside the sphere of Roman influence. It was not a uniform defensive work but its eastern end, that is to say, the Newcastle end, was always the stronger and for many miles to the west of Newcastle the Wall was 20-ft thick, tapering down to about 8-ft thick in the central sections. To the west of the Irthing valley it was originally constructed of turf, though stone was substituted later. There was a ditch in front of the Wall, that is to say, on the Scottish side, and a vallum (a ditch and bank) on the English side to provide a second line of defence. In many parts of the Wall it is possible to see clearly the remains of both these features. Some miles to the south there was a military road which served the fortresses along the Wall and the course of this also is known and in places on our route has been built up into a modern highway.

The Wall not only presented a passive defence to attacking tribes but at intervals along it active points of resistance. There was a mile castle at intervals of approximately one Roman mile (considerably shorter than an English mile) and two turrets placed at equal distances between the mile castles, while the occasional forts were the permanent headquarters of the legionaries who guarded the Wall. The greatest possible tribute to this remarkable feat of military engineering is that it was never taken by storm. The only times when the Scottish tribes overran it was when for one reason or another the legionaries had been recalled to York or further south and the forts and mile castles were left unguarded. It continued to be the main defence of the Roman province until the end of the fourth century, when the Roman troops were finally withdrawn to defend the frontiers of empire nearer Rome.

It is, practically speaking, impossible to drive along the Wall and visit the numerous sites which have been excavated or preserved by the Ministry of Works in a single day. Indeed, the tour which follows, which does not exceed 90 miles from central Newcastle and back, has enough of interest in it to last far more than a single day. It would be better divided into two or even

three. It takes us as far as the Cumberland boundary. Beyond
that, apart from one or two significant exceptions, the remains of
the wall are less interesting, but the route given in Chapter 8
which covers the way from Gilsland to Carlisle can be followed
as a continuation of this route to include the whole of the Roman
Wall that can be seen from a car.

Right from the beginning of the tour, which leaves Newcastle
by A69, we are on or near the course of the Wall. Did you know,
for instance, that there was a Roman temple within the boundaries of Newcastle? Extraordinarily few do. It is one of two
sites very well worth finding on the way out. The temple is
signposted on a post beside A69 at Benwell down Weidner Road.
The temple is really only 200 yards from the main road but
difficult to find. We take the first turning on the right, Westholme
Road, off Weidner Road, then the first on the left, Broomridge
Avenue, and there is the temple on our left, beautifully reconstructed, with the casts of two original altars dating from the
latter part of the second century. The temple is dedicated to the
Celtic god Antenocitius and gives a remarkably accurate picture
of what a Roman temple must have looked like in the second
century. One only has to imagine the walls and the roof, which
would have been fairly plain.

The second site is less than a quarter of a mile away. To reach
it we return to the main road, turn left then left again in Denhill
Park, which is opposite a high television aerial. We shall find it
at the lower end of this modern suburban development. Here
there is a causeway which carried a metalled road over the ditch
of the vallum leading to the fort of Condercum. Some of the
original stones are preserved, including the west pier of the
bridge gate.

Continuing along A69 we shall find no less than three stretches
of the Wall between here and Heddon on the Wall. The first is
at East Denton—70 yards long and including a turret, the second
at West Denton also about 70 yards long, and only about an
eighth of a mile beyond the former. This is particularly interesting
because it retains some of the giant stones which were characteristic of the east end of the Wall.

Finally, at the approach to Heddon on the Wall there is a fine
stretch more than 250 yards long composed of the original
stones though not built up to its original height. The Wall is

complete with the protective ditch, which is exceptionally well marked at this point.

At Heddon on the Wall we bear right for Chollerford, with the vallum on our left and the ditch on our right. Amazingly the original of this road was built by General Wade, that famous warrior and road engineer, on the very site of the Wall. General Wade cut down the Wall to its base and used the stones as a valuable foundation of the road. So we can reasonably say that we are actually riding on the Wall. As we drive along we shall pass many farmhouses and barns whose fabric is composed wholly or partly of stones taken from the Wall, for stone robbers were rife throughout the Middle Ages right down to the nineteenth century. The Wall was regarded as a ready-made quarry and its stones carted away for building whenever it was convenient. No one said the stone robbers nay. Were it not for this fact the greater part of the Wall would be standing to this day.

There is nothing very significant to see for a few miles, then at the Whittledene reservoir we turn left for Newton, passing a ruined pele tower, which is attached to later farm buildings like so many in this part of the country. At the first junction we go forward in a narrow lane for Corbridge and continue right into Corbridge on this pleasant road which passes through peaceful undulating country looking left and ahead into the Tyne valley, to which we gradually descend, with the Durham moors standing out magnificently on a clear day on the further side of the valley.

It is well worth neglecting the first turning signposted to Corstopitum and going into the town, which is dominated by the church and the ancient fortified vicarage in the churchyard. In the picturesque market square we shall find the steps of the old market cross crowned by a later iron shaft and cross erected by Hugh Percy, Duke of Northumberland, in 1813, and near it a conical pump and horse trough, erected at the expense of the same benefactor two years later. Appropriately, though horses are scarce in this part of Northumberland, the trough is still filled and the pump is crowned by a lamp and signposts.

We leave Corbridge by the Otterburn road, bearing left by the 'Wheatsheaf' hotel and left again on the Hexham road for Corstopitum. Although this is strictly speaking not part of the Wall defences it was built in conjunction with the Wall as a main supply base. Its remains, though fragmentary, are remarkably revealing and show clearly the development of a Roman supply base which became a civil town between the first and third centuries A.D.

We continue beyond Corstopitum on the same road for nearly two miles along the Tyne valley, then turn right for Anick when we are just within sight of Hexham ahead, thereafter going forward for Oakwood. After passing Oakwood post office and a row of houses we turn right for Sandhoe and continue straight ahead on the Sandhoe road, a steep hill road. Halfway up the hill, however, we turn left in an obscure turning for Acomb, and right at the next crossroads, about a quarter of a mile further going forward over yet another crossroads for Codlaw Hill. This is a complicated but not too difficult route to follow. Our last road is a straight high road which takes us back to the course of the Wall. We turn left at a group of farms by a wood half a mile short of it, crossing a well-marked section of the vallum and ditch just before reaching the main road, in which we turn left.

Just beyond Planetrees Farm on our left 50 yards of the Wall stand out clearly in a field beside the road, forming a natural feature of the countryside all the more memorable because of the long view up the Tyne valley which it commands. At the foot of the hill our way is straight ahead for Chollerford but it is worth making a short detour on the Hexham road to see the Brunton turret, one of the best preserved on the line of the Wall, and another 70 yards of the Wall which is reached by an easy footpath from the Hexham road.

Returning, we cross the North Tyne at one of its loveliest reaches, turning left on B6318 for Carlisle and soon reaching the car park for Chesters, or, as it is more properly known, Cilurnum, one of the principal Roman forts along the Wall. The remains are of a fort which it is estimated accommodated more than 500 men. It has been possible to reconstruct the foundations of most of the principal buildings, including the barracks and the bath houses, which were a feature of every Roman installation.

Now our road takes us along the Carlisle road towards Housesteads. As we enter the Northumberland National Park the vallum and ditch are very clearly marked on the left of the road and there are fragmentary (unadopted) parts of the Wall equally clearly visible on the right. Soon a sign shows the way to a temple of Mithras on our left, a temple which was outside the fort of Procolitia and probably dates from the third century.

A capacious car park serves Housesteads but it is a stiff walk to the fort, the walls of which can be seen from the road, as well as the cultivation terraces just to the south of it. Housesteads has been thoroughly excavated. It was certainly a fort which in its heyday was manned by a thousand men. The more energetic will walk from this car park up to the fort, see the section of the Wall at Sewingshields, and walk to the west past another minor fort as far as the Winshields Crag, traversing a part of the Wall which reaches its highest altitude, almost 1,250 ft above sea-level, with really outstanding views from the cliffs over the Border country, Crag Lough a prominent feature at the foot of the sheer drop. The crags are part of the Whin Sill, described earlier.

If we are less energetic we shall visit Housesteads, then drive along another 2 miles towards Carlisle, turning right for Winshields Crag, where there is another good car park and access to the Wall, which itself is used as a footpath leading towards Housesteads fort. So one is not committed to any particular distance and certainly sees the best of the scenery as well as the finest part of the Wall.

To the west of this point, however, as far as the Cumberland boundary, the only way to see the Wall is on foot. Though the Wall itself is fragmentary the scenery is so magnificent that anyone who feels equal to a 5-mile walk should try it. There is no easy circular route, though one can walk west from Winshields Crag for about two miles until one strikes a road again, then return right-handed by it to the car park. But it is almost seven miles from Winshields to the point where the Wall returns to the neighbourhood of a main road at Greenhead.

Whatever we decide to do, we drive on ultimately past the car park at Winshields Crag and at a T-junction turn left for Halt-whistle, soon recrossing the Whin Sill and the Wall and emerging on a major road, B6318, in which we turn right and after a mile at the 'Mile Castle' inn left, still making for Haltwhistle, and soon descending to the banks of the South Tyne. There is no need to go through the rambling town of Haltwhistle, the principal feature of which is its fine medieval church. Instead if we turn left at the first major road on approaching it we avoid it almost

entirely, crossing in a few yards a second major road for Melk-
ridge, with the gorge of the South Tyne on our right, a most
exciting road even although at times it approaches to within less
than 100 yards of the trunk road. We follow the banks of the
South Tyne, with unobstructed views into the valley for nearly
three miles but beyond Redburn briefly join the main road,
going forward but leaving it in 100 yards by the first turning on
the left, which is currently unsignposted, beside a group of houses.

Then we turn right in half a mile for Borcorvicum (even the
Northumbrian roadmakers have a feeling for their Roman
heritage), continuing forward for it at a subsequent junction.
In about a mile and a half, after a series of outstanding views, we
veer right for Newbrough and join the Roman road which served
the fortresses along the Wall. The Roman origin of this road is
certainly not in doubt: it is straight and takes us after 6 scenic
miles through Newbrough, where we follow the Hexham
signposts, passing the classical town hall dated 1876 on our left.

At the next junction we go forward for Chollerford, then left
on B6319. We drop gently to the valley of the North Tyne and
cross it at Chollerford by B6318, turning left at the subsequent
crossroads, and following briefly the course of the North Tyne
towards Chollerton. At an obscure unsignposted turn by a bun-
galow, however, we turn right, leaving the river and passing under
a railway bridge in a few yards. After half a mile we pass a
ruined pele tower half hidden by farm buildings on our right
and at a major road turn right for just over a mile, then turn left
near the top of a hill where the way is signposted Matfen. So we
pass the B.B.C. transmitting station and drive on for Great
Whittington, turning left at the next T-junction and right after
a quarter of a mile at a T-junction into Matfen.

Matfen is a striking place, one of the prettiest villages in
Northumberland. Its spired church is its centrepiece and its
spacious village green, backed by eighteenth- and early nineteenth-
century houses, makes a highly agreeable composition. Here we
turn left for Stamfordham, following the signposts to it, and find
another village built round a spacious green, with a classical
market cross and many old houses. At the end of the green we
bear right for Newcastle. Afterwards the signposts do not fail
us, though the way is still through country scenes, parklands and
meadows and ploughed fields, until Newburn colliery abruptly

reminds us that we are approaching a great industrial city and we reach its suburbs about four miles from the centre.

The North Tyne is a highlight of Northumberland's scenery although it is frequently overlooked, partly because it lacks the dramatic interludes of the South Tyne. But it is just as attractive as the South Tyne for most of its length and makes a genuinely outstanding objective for a modest tour from the Tyneside towns, or indeed from most of County Durham. It rises only a few miles from the Scottish Border; its upper reaches are in the great Kielder Forest, which we explore as part of a tour described in the next chapter. Indeed the tour through the Kielder Forest Park and back through Redesdale Forest Park may be regarded as an extension of the present tour. What we set out to do now is to follow the course of the North Tyne as far as the approach to the Kielder Forest Park well upstream from Bellingham, then take a tortuous but often beautiful way across the moors, skirting Harwood Forest and returning to Tyneside through the quiet pastoral scenery round Belsay. The total length is about 105 miles from central Newcastle, mostly on narrow but not difficult roads. The majority of motorists will find it an ideal length for a summer afternoon and evening, and far enough for a long day's tour.

If we are starting from Newcastle the most convenient exit from the city is by A696, which we follow as far as Ponteland, visited on another tour. Here we continue for a further mile on the main road, passing a ruined pele tower on our right just beyond the turn to the church. Then we turn left on a narrow road signposted Milbourne, passing through a number of patches of informal woodland before reaching a junction, at which we bear left for Milbourne Hall, turning right where the road to the Hall is on our left, and left again just beyond the church at a staggered crossroads.

Here our way is signposted Stamfordham. At the next T-junction we turn right away from Ponteland (naturally) emerging on an open road which because of its low hedges commands unrestricted views and is a joy to drive along. On reaching a major road we bear right where a signpost shows Capheaton and follow this way past a large farm group. Next we go straight on in a minor road where the way is still signposted Capheaton to the next crossroads, where we turn left for Ingoe and Ryal.

This road is bordered by a belt of pine trees but soon emerges on Ingoe Moor, a rather bleak contrast with the mainly fertile and smiling lowlands exceeding an elevation of 750 ft. However, the views to the right across Rothbury Forest to the Cheviot are outstanding. At the turn to Ingoe village we go straight on and at the next junction bear left for Ryal, now temporarily turning south and looking across the Tyne valley to the Durham moors, a series of quite superb views. When we reach Ryal crossroads we turn right on a major road for Hallington and begin a series of steep descents which carry us ultimately to the valley of the North Tyne.

We cross a crossroads at the foot of one hill for Barrasford and continue to a main road, crossing it into another major road, at the sign of the 'Barrasford Arms', forking right for Barrasford after a long mile then bearing right at a subsequent T-junction. So we reach Barrasford, a Tyneside village of considerable charm commanding a fine view of Haughton Castle across the river. The latter is one of the finest of the tower houses or pele towers in Northumberland and is best seen perhaps just before we reach the centre of the village, where it is a dominating feature of the landscape.

For the next twelve miles or more our road is parallel with and close to the course of the North Tyne. The river is by no means always visible though here and there its course can be seen ahead of us. But always there is the lush beauty of the valley with its well-wooded landscapes, its occasional fine houses, and the hills rising gently to low summits from either bank. We pass the Jacobean manor-house of Chipchase Castle on our left, and eventually cross the river into Wark. It comes as a real surprise to find how broad it is at this point. Normally a gently flowing river after heavy rain in the Border moorlands it can produce a brown spate of water carrying wood and rock debris over a series of tiny cascades which give it an appearance of real anger and power.

Wark is a picturesque village centred round a square green, an admirable composition, though few of the houses are really distinguished in themselves. Beyond it we bear right on B6320 for Bellingham, now closely following the west bank of the river and soon crossing the Houxty burn near its confluence with the parent river. There are fine views up the valley of the Houxty and about here particularly long views over the valley of the

Tyne towards Redesdale, for the valley of the Rede joins that of the Tyne between here and Bellingham. We shall be visiting Bellingham on another tour. So on this occasion just beyond the town sign on its outskirts we turn left for Kielder, soon crossing a tributary, the Chirdon burn, by an old stone bridge. Now we take the first opportunity to cross the Tyne by a massive metal bridge, about a quarter of a mile beyond, where the way ahead is signposted Falstone. After another quarter of a mile we cross the Tarset burn, bearing round to the left after that and continuing to a major road which we cross for Greenhaugh.

This is the end of our North Tyne tour but by no means the end of the interesting and often lovely country which our way traverses. Beyond Greenhaugh we turn right for High Green and continue over the moors for some miles to a major road in which our way is briefly to the right as far as a crossroads, where we turn left for Otterburn, entering this famous centre of Redesdale past the equally famous Otterburn Mill.

There we turn right for Newcastle but soon bear left on B6341 for Rothbury as far as Elsdon, where we turn right for Newcastle again, and make a point of seeing the fine old pele tower which was once the rectory, and the medieval church which retains much of its exquisite tracery and is in many ways one of the most interesting in this part of the country. After crossing Elsdon green, which is almost surrounded by graceful houses, and crossing a stream, the Elsdon burn, we bear left for Cambo, soon leaving the valley behind us and climbing on to bare moors where for some distance we ride above the 1,000-ft contour. As we skirt the National Trust property of Wallington the last of the forbidding gibbets remaining in the country is a stern reminder of more troubled days when life was counted less highly than it is now.

The thickets and plantations of Harwood Forest are beside us for the next 3 miles, almost until we turn right for Cambo, joining a wider road over lower but still pleasant pastoral country in which the moors are little more than a memory, even though we are still over 700 ft above sea-level, and descend very gradually. After a long mile we turn right towards Knowesgate with the unmistakable outline of Rothbury Forest a prominent landmark on our right.

On reaching the crossroads with A696 we cross the main road

for Woodburn over another fine breezy plateau and bear left at
the first signpost for Redesmouth. This is a gated road, a very
lonely one, soon bringing us to the lovely Sweethope reservoir.
When we leave it behind us the terrain for a time becomes sterner,
with numerous rock outcrops, a rugged contrast with the peaceful
and lovely man-made scenery of the lake. Even sheep seem few
and far between on this part of the route, which is made memorable chiefly by the magnificent views into Redesdale and the North
Tyne valley.

On reaching a major road we turn left for Corbridge, continuing to a point just past the 'Tone' inn, where we bear left on
a tiny road which is signposted Thockrington and Kirkwhelping-
ton. We neglect a right turn in half a mile but at the next fork
bear right for Thockrington, soon reaching the Colt Crag
reservoir, another beautiful man-made stretch of water, extraordinarily little visited for a beauty spot so near a great industrial
area. We go through two gates and turn sharp left in the midst
of moorland about 200 yards beyond the crossing of the reservoir
for Thockrington, soon coming to the only signs of the village,
a solitary little church, Norman and heavily buttressed, high on
a rock outcrop, and the scattered farmhouses in the vicinity.
After that we continue along a high moorland road, though
mature trees and even hawthorn bushes occur by the wayside.
Then on reaching a major road, A6079, we turn left in it for
Kirkharle, passing an ancient ruined dovecot on the hill to our right.

Now we are approaching the lowlands. Our road becomes
wholly tree-lined, the landscape more and more cultivated with
every mile we go. We pass Bavington Hall and park, and beyond
it go straight on for Newcastle. At the next junction, however,
we leave the wider road for the lesser way straight ahead
towards Capheaton, driving down a venerable avenue and continuing as far as the crossroads on the outskirts of the village,
where we turn right for Stamfordham, and at the next T-junction
bear left for Belsay, going forward beside the park wall.

Belsay is not open to the public but there are incomparable
views of the handsome wooded park and one fine glimpse of its
ancient pele tower among the trees. It makes a memorable
ending to this tour as we reach A696 again at Belsay village and
take the direct way back to Newcastle and the other Tyneside
towns.

CHAPTER FOUR

THE FORESTS OF THE BORDER COUNTRY

THE THREE ROUTES in this chapter take us first to the Forest of Rothbury, which is divided into two by the lovely valley of the Coquet, the second to the Forest of the Cheviot, or rather as near the summit of the Cheviot Hills as it is possible to drive a car, the third to the great new forest which has changed the face of the land on the borders of England and Scotland between Deadwater and Carter Bar including Peel Fell and Carter Fell, both of which approach 2,000 ft above sea-level.

The word 'forest' does not strictly connote trees but was originally the name of medieval hunting preserves in which the laws were stringent to prevent the poaching of game by people living in the settlements in the forest or on its edge. Some of the great forests of the Middle Ages were treeless, such as the Forest of Skiddaw, others like the New Forest not nearly so well afforested as now. All were regarded as tracts of country which could not make a worthwhile contribution to the economy, either because of the poverty of the soil or because of the exposed nature of the terrain.

Two of the three forests we explore are exceptionally well wooded though the woods are recent and have changed the face of the countryside within living memory. The Forest of the Cheviot, however, the hills and fells which fan out from the volcanic peak of this border mountain, is treeless. But Rothbury Forest, which retains many of its medieval features in the bold rocky slopes and outcrops of the high ground, contains also some of the most beautiful wooded country in Northumberland, especially round the market town of Rothbury which is its true capital. The valley of the Coquet is smiling with crops and sheep pasture over all but the very roughest part of the high ground. Our third forest, to the west, is a brainchild of the Forestry Commission. The tireless work of those who have laboured for years to bring a green cover to this boggy and peaty wilderness

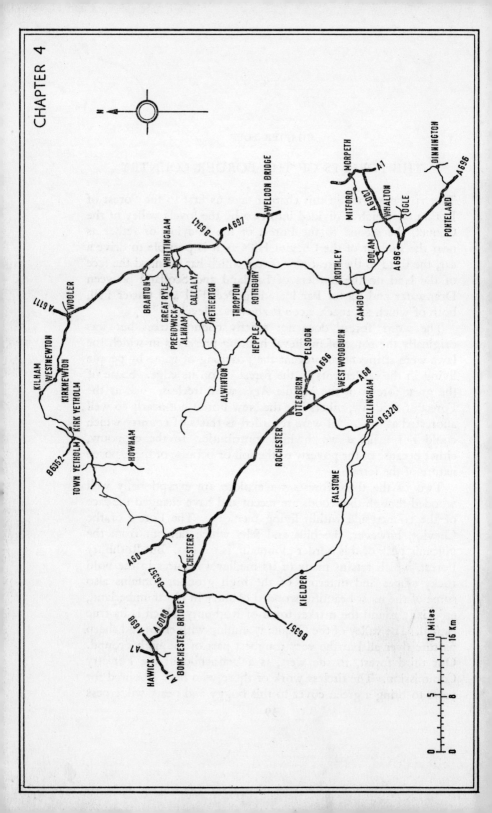

Landscape near the head of East Allendale.   (Chapter 3.)

Part of the reconstructed Roman Wall at Winshields Crag.   (Chapter 3.)

The river Coquet near Rothbury.　(Chapter 4.)

The head of East Allendale.　(Chapter 3.)

has succeeded beyond expectation. Now the road which not so many years ago was no more than a track crossing the forest from Wark into the lowlands of Scotland commands vistas of growing plantations which represent the wealth of tomorrow. Altogether the three rides are in remarkable contrast.

The first tour is an easy round from Newcastle of about 100 miles. The other two can also be undertaken from Newcastle in a single day but make long days' motoring. It is clearly preferable to attempt the circuit of the Cheviot from a centre such as Wooler or Bamburgh, while the best centres for the third are Wark and Otterburn.

For our tour to Rothbury, then, we leave Newcastle by the Great North Road, A1, crossing the Town Moor, and continuing towards Morpeth until we are 3½ miles from Newcastle centre. As our turning is obscure we shall welcome a clue given by the 'Three Mile' inn, which is just opposite the entrance to a golf club. Barely half a mile further we turn left in Brunton Lane beside a garage and right at a major road T-junction, bearing left at the next junction for Dinnington.

Dinnington has the feel of Newcastle about it but beyond it we might be fifty miles from the nearest large town as we go on for Ponteland through quiet landscapes where the views are always to the distant backcloth of Rothbury Forest less than twenty-five miles away. On a clear day the long line of the Border hills can be seen.

At a major road, by Prestwick Road End, our way is to the right into Ponteland, where we turn right for Morpeth, passing the church, claimed to be one of the finest churches in Northumberland . It certainly has an exceptionally beautiful Norman tower. Just opposite, the 'Blackbird' inn incorporates part of an old mansion which has been singularly little altered by conversion into a hostelry. Near the end of the village we bear left and at a T-junction by the entrance to Kirkley Hall left again for Ogle and Whalton. We follow the signposts to both but find little to detain us in Ogle, though Whalton has another fine church with several Norman features and shows very clearly the evolution of a later medieval church from a Norman one. The very elaborate design of the pier of the north chancel arch is specially beautiful and incorporates four lovely carved heads and a profusion of dogtooth moulding more fully developed here perhaps than in any other church, certainly in the north country.

The picturesque village is just beyond the church. In it we turn left past a long row of stone houses fringed by a tree-shaded green. Just past the 'Beresford Arms' we turn right for Meldon, going forward for Bolam at a subsequent signposted junction, driving through parkland with many fine and venerable trees, and soon catching a glimpse of the Saxon tower of Bolam church. At a T-junction in the midst of woodlands we turn left along a road fringed with rhododendron bushes, passing a large lake set in the midst of the woodlands and at the junction beyond this turn right for Cambo and Scots Gap.

For a time we follow the further shore of the lake and go forward at a subsequent junction for Scots Gap. We drive up the green Wansbeck valley for over a mile after crossing the river, then turn right for Cambo and Rothbury through the estate of Wallington Hall, a National Trust property which is open to the public on summer weekend and Wednesday afternoons, a splendid seventeenth- and eighteenth-century building with later additions. If it is not open when we pass there is a grand view of it from the road. A feature which intrigues many people who pass is the four beasts' heads which seem to be springing out of the lawn. These originally decorated one of the City gates of London and are said to have been used as ballast on coastal colliers from London to Tynemouth.

We pass the 'Clock Tower' restaurant, which is part of the former stables of the hall, and at the next crossroads go forward once more for Cambo and Scots Gap, turning right in Cambo for the latter and there, just after crossing a railway, bear left for Rothley. So we pass the impressive group of rocks known as Rothley Crags, one of the most conspicuous outcrops in the whole of the Rothbury Forest area.

We go forward for Rothbury at subsequent turnings, passing the pretty Rothley lakes, one on each side of the road, and exceeding the 800-ft contour at the highest point, with the high ridge of the forest to the left and ahead of us. After a mile or two we begin to descend steeply to cross the Forest burn deep in a wooded combe. Just beyond the crossing we pass the 'Crown and Thistle' inn and one mile beyond this, where there is the characteristic sign of the Northumberland Forest Park, we turn left in a minor unsignposted road which climbs over the fells and commands splendid views of Coquetdale as it descends the further side.

When we reach another road we bear left by a farm group, passing a ruined pele tower (every farm in this countryside had its pele during the Middle Ages). At the next junction we go forward for Little Tosson and continue on this byway for nearly three miles, always near the course of the Coquet, to a junction with B6341. Here we turn right for Hepple, crossing the Coquet at one of its loveliest reaches and passing another ruined pele tower in Hepple. We follow the B road, which carries very little traffic, as far as Thropton and there on the further side of a stream turn left for Whittingham and Callaly, climbing once more until we are looking from the edge of Rothbury Forest to the rugged mass of the Cheviot. Callaly Castle is signposted a short distance to the left of the road, another historic home open to the public on summer weekend afternoons, its main feature a late seventeenth-century mansion not unlike Wallington Hall, with a thirteenth-century pele tower in a state of excellent preservation.

Whittingham, too, has a fine pele tower which in the nineteenth century served as an almshouse and still looks capable of serving as a modern residence. There is a fountain at the road junction near the end of the village. Here we bear right for Alnwick past the 'Castle' inn and at the Bridge of Aln turn right on A697, which is signposted Newcastle, following it for two or three miles to a crossroads where we turn right on B6341 into Rothbury. That is a ride which will long remain in the memory, through some of the finest scenery of Rothbury Forest, which gives an air of spaciousness greater even than most moorland roads, though we only reach just over 900 ft at the highest point.

Soon we begin to descend into Coquetdale, entering dense woodlands and passing the entrance to Cragside. Its famous and lovely gardens are open daily including Sundays and are at their finest when the rhododendrons are in bloom. Rothbury is a charming little riverside town, its church attractive though much restored dominating the green and the rows of stone houses, which look across the main street to the high shaded bank on which is the chief shopping thoroughfare. The bridge, a very ancient one, is a disappointment because it has been so cruelly

widened but the river upstream and downstream has real beauty
and distinction.

We retrace our way for a quarter of a mile towards Cragside
then fork right for Newcastle alongside the Coquet to Weldon
Bridge on A697, passing the lane which leads to Brinkburn
Priory on our right. At Weldon Bridge by the 'Anglers Arms'
we turn right towards Morpeth but after just half a mile turn
right again for Todburn, so continuing the series of attractive
byways which have formed the greater part of the route. The
Cheviot and Rothbury Forest are receding but they still dominate
the landscapes. On reaching a wider road we go forward by the
small group of houses which comprise Todburn, then follow a
virtually straight course for several miles along a pleasant
tree-lined road.

We must neglect various beguiling side turnings but after the
right turn to Beacon Hill, where we go forward again (signposted Morpeth) and continue for another mile then veer right
at a fork for Benridge Moor, and at a subsequent junction go
forward again where the way is once more signposted Morpeth.
We turn left for Mitford and Morpeth at a T-junction and right
for Mitford at a subsequent junction. Then in the wooded gorge
of the river Font we turn right in a major road, cross a stone
bridge, and now in the gorge of the Wansbeck turn left after a
quarter of a mile into an obscure turning which leads to old
Mitford.

This is the last place of real interest on our tour but by no
means the least memorable. The substantial fragments of the
castle are on a mound on one side of the road, impressive if only
because of their commanding situation. The fragments of the
Carolean manor-house of the Mitfords can be seen from the
churchyard, while the church itself has a splendid Early English
chancel as well as Norman arches and columns in the nave and
a Norman priest's door beautifully moulded.

Shortly beyond this point we turn left for Gubeon, going
forward over a major crossroads for Kirkley, then left in a wood
for Tranwell, bearing right at a wider road for Stannington.
Now it is largely a matter of personal preference and available
time which way we follow. The Great North Road is never far
from us on our left. We can join at any point and complete our
journey swiftly and easily. To continue on byways as nearly as

possible to Newcastle's centre we follow the Stannington sign-posts at the next two junctions but at a double junction (one road going left and the other right) where the Stannington road goes left we bear right, and right again shortly at a T-junction, crossing the river Blyth in about a mile by a hogback bridge and continuing to another junction where the way is to the left for Seaton burn, but right again soon afterwards for Dinnington. This brings us back to our outward way and we can drive on through Dinnington, after that taking a turning on the left for Newcastle. Here though our goal is only 6 miles distant we are still in open country with scarcely a sign of the great metropolis.

The next tour, which takes us to the Kielder Forest Park and the Redesdale Forest Park, two of the largest modern forest parks in England, can be treated by many readers as a projection of the tour from Newcastle to Wark and the upper North Tyne. If the route described in Chapter 3 is followed to the point where we cross the Tyne and instead of crossing it go straight on, we shall be in Kielder Forest within three or four miles. Then on the completion of the tour at Otterburn we can return direct to Newcastle by A696. That will give a total mileage of no more than 160 miles, by no means an impossible assignment for a long summer's day, especially as the tour is mainly of scenic interest and there are fewer places than usual where one feels the urge to leave the car and explore an historic house or a church or any of the other interesting features which we find on most of our tours.

When we cross the Scottish boundary we have a sight of Hermitage Castle, an admirable example of a Border fortress, now open to the public, and also drive through the border town of Hawick. Otherwise the tour alternates mainly between moor-land and forest, with beauty in every mile and real distinction in many parts of it. Clearly if it is possible, however, it is better to treat the tour on its own merits, starting either from Otterburn or Bellingham, or for that matter from Hawick. The description is as from Otterburn though the directions are precisely the same from the other two. Then the total distance is just over 90 miles, ideal for an afternoon and evening on holiday, or a whole day's tour with leisurely stops at some of the finest viewpoints along the course of the upper Tyne and in the midst of the forests, where in spite of the need to take precautions against fire picnic places are provided and there is a hearty welcome for the wayfarer.

If the start is at Otterburn we follow the Newcastle road, A696, for about two miles then turn right for East Woodburn along a fine moorland road. There is a sense of real spaciousness as we look over the vast landscape to the Border hills, with the river Rede which joins the Tyne near Bellingham winding its way through the valley below us. In East Woodburn, a compact hamlet of pleasant cottages, we turn right, following the course of the Rede and passing the little church on our left. After descending close to the waterway of the Rede we reach a major road, A68, in which we turn right briefly towards Bellingham, crossing the Rede at West Woodburn then immediately turning left opposite the 'Bay Horse' hotel.

It is a straightforward 4 miles from here to Bellingham, mainly along the valley of the Rede and then into the valley of the North Tyne, which we approach over a flat-topped ridge. And so into Bellingham, a good place for Tyneside motorists to join the route. We go under the railway bridge and cross a small tributary stream, turning left immediately on B6320 through the town's most attractive centre, a tiny market square from which radiate tree-lined streets of pleasant houses underlining the prosperity of a place which had its heyday more than a hundred years ago and has lived on to play the part of a small country town in the modern economy. We leave B6320 at the end of the town, going forward on a minor road for Falstone where the major road bends sharp left, and for the next few miles follow the north bank of the North Tyne, entering on the way the North-umberland National Park. It is an exceptionally lovely ride with many glimpses of the still broad river close beside us and one splendid view where we can see it winding through the country-side ahead of us.

At the first crossroads we turn left for Falstone, crossing the Tarset burn, a tributary, then the North Tyne itself. On the further side we turn right for Falstone. The country gradually becomes more rugged, the river if possible lovelier as it flows down from the hills over a bed covered in large stones and rocks which produce a thousand tiny cascades. As we enter the Border Forest Park of Kielder conifer forests seem to fill the whole landscape on both banks of the river and up the hillsides as far as eye can reach. But we can still see the Tyne at intervals winding along the valley on our right.

When we emerge from the woods and reach an unobstructed viewpoint Peel Fell (1,975 ft) and Carter Fell (1,815 ft), two of the highest Border hills west of the Cheviot, are seen rearing their flat-topped heads on our right, with the woods climbing to the very summit of Peel Fell. There are a few new forestry settlements, especially at Kielder itself, but their gaily painted houses make a pleasant interlude in the green of the forest lands, and we pass the little church of Kielder in the forest, its church-yard beautified by shapely Irish yews. Incidentally, Kielder Border Forest Park had the distinction of inaugurating the first trailside museum in the country. It is open to the public and is situated at the entrance to the Lewisburn Camping site.

At one point our road is signposted Newcastleton and we cross the infant Tyne before coming out on the virgin moors on the Scottish side of the Border, almost treeless in contrast with the forest land through which we have driven. We continue over the low pass which separates the headwaters of the North Tyne from those of the Liddel Water and shortly reach B6357, in which our way is to the left for Canonbie for several miles until a turning on the right is signposted Hermitage Castle.

In clear weather we have a glimpse of the Lake District mountains through a gap in the hills. Then on reaching B6399 we go forward for Hawick but make a short detour to see Hermitage Castle, which is still well signposted. It is a splendid ruin which was once a stronghold of the Douglases. It figures in the romantic and tragic story of Mary, Queen of Scots, who came here from Jedburgh to see Bothwell in 1566 and almost died of a fever contracted, it is said, as a result of her long and arduous ride. Although it is in ruins today enough has survived to make it possible to reconstruct a large part of the medieval stronghold in the mind's eye.

Resuming our way to Hawick on B6399, we drive over many miles of real moorland road, the marshy ground on which grows only rank grass providing no more than rough pasturage for a few sheep. But there are grand views as we reach the summit of the pass and many minor peaks break up the smooth outline of the moors.

Hawick is at once one of the most historic Border towns and

today the largest town of Roxburghshire, with a prosperous manufacturing industry, mostly in wool and woollen yarns. Its most precious memory is of the day in 1514 after Flodden when a detachment of Hawick young men defeated a company of English soldiers, capturing their banner, an event which is celebrated with tremendous enthusiasm at the Riding of the Marches early in June, giving Hawick a real and prominent place in Scottish folklore. The equestrian monument at the east end of the High Street is to the 'Callants' of Hawick, i.e. the youths, who carried out this daring deed with such success. Of the very few old buildings part of the 'Tower' hotel dates from the sixteenth century and is said to be the only building which was not burnt to the ground during the English attack of 1570. The 'Tolbooth' in the High Street which looks so very baronial, is relatively modern. The church, which we pass on our way into the town, is a fair example of the eighteenth-century churches of southern Scotland.

We drive the whole length of the High Street past the Tolbooth and fork right by the Callants memorial on A698 for Kelso, then turn right on A6088 for Bonchester Bridge, a wonderfully quiet road for an A road, which gives good views of the rugged outliers of the Cheviot. Later the whole panorama of the Border hills on the Scottish side is spread before us.

At Bonchester Bridge we bear right for Newcastle. As we ascend the view retrospectively is most impressive and reaches to the valley of the Tweed and the Tweedsmuir Hills. At Chesters we turn right again for Newcastle. For mile after mile one has to search the landscape carefully to find a single farmhouse. Then just after joining A68 we reach the summit at Carter Bar and return into England at the site of the last Scottish-English Border affray in 1575.

Our road reaches 1,370 ft but it gives the impression of being much higher. As we begin the descent into Redesdale we soon see the infant Rede on our right, its course dammed to form the Catcleugh reservoir before it resumes its long journey to the North Tyne. Our road runs the whole length of the reservoir, a beautiful stretch of water half surrounded by belts of conifers. At its foot we enter the Redesdale Forest Park and pass the Byrness forestry settlement. Now, as in Kielder Forest, the slopes on either side are completely covered in trees, a most

impressive sight and perhaps the justification of man's handi-
work, not only in drawing wealth from intractable nature but in
actually improving on nature's pattern. Before the reservoir and
the forests became dominant features of the landscape this was a
dreary valley, boggy and featureless.

The return to Otterburn is through Rochester village and past
the site of the battle of Otterburn, known as Chevy Chase and
fought in 1388. There is a monument of the battle in the form of
an obelisk known as the Percy Cross, a modern one on the site of
an earlier one, about 100 yards to the left of the road in a small
wood. Bearing left on A696, we reach the hotels and petrol
stations of Otterburn and quite suddenly we seem very far from
the forests and moors through which we have driven for most
of the day.

The last tour in this chapter, which takes us round the Cheviot
as nearly as possible as one can drive to it by car, is another
which can be undertaken in a single day by Tyneside motorists
but is far far better treated as a tour in its own right, starting and
finishing either at Otterburn, like the previous one, or at Wooler,
or at any of the villages along the route which have accommodation, such as Yetholm. If the start is made at Jedburgh or Hawick,
both places that sound many miles away from the Cheviot, the
additional mileage is negligible.

If it is treated as a day tour from Tyneside, the best way of
approach is by A696 as far as Otterburn, while the return can be
made by main road from any point after Wooler, which is on
A697, via Morpeth and A1, perhaps leaving the second part of the
tour up the Coquet valley into the very heart of the moors for
another occasion. The distance from Tyneside and back is not
much more than 160 miles to complete either tour. The route
described from Otterburn or Wooler, making the complete
circuit of the Cheviot and ascending the gorge of the Coquet as
far as it is possible to go works out at about 120 miles and is
perhaps the finest of border tours. Many of the roads are surprisingly good having regard to the terrain and the fact that they
do no more than link scattered hamlets or farm with farm makes
for a slightly higher average speed than on most of our tours.

Our way takes us into the very heart of the Cheviot moors at
many places and occasionally to places where it is no more than
five or six miles' walking to the summit, with a good track or

footpath to begin the journey. These look misleadingly simple when you can see the summit of the hill ahead of you but become rather wearisome and certainly tiring when you come to the end of the path and emerge on the boggy upper slopes with very little to guide you to the summit (which is always tantalisingly out of sight in the last mile or two) except your sense of direction and a compass. I feel that the ascent of the Cheviot, more than that of most of the highest hills of England and southern Scotland, is a walk for the true enthusiast rather than the 'amateur'. Yet the scenery in the foothills is the equal of that in any mountainous part of England, not excluding the Lake District; to see that is precisely our aim today.

If our start is from Otterburn we drive first to Carter Bar on A696 and A68 (there is no alternative), the same way, in fact, in reverse as we traversed at the end of the last tour. However, it is a grand ride of which one never tires. We pass the traditional last 'house' in England, the 'Redesdale Arms', which prominently displays its tidings. Travellers in this direction may be surprised to find in the midst of the forest several miles further up the road the 'Byrness' hotel, which serves the forestry village and has an admirable 'Border Bar'. So 'you pays your money and takes your choice'.

After crossing the Border we turn left on A6088. A68 would be a shorter way but the other is such a superlatively fine road that we cannot bear to omit it. The views seem even better over southern Scotland in this direction than they do going south. At the first signposted crossroads, which we reach after about five miles in the village of Chesters, we turn right for Camptown. This is our first small byway on the route and a very lovely one it is, winding uphill between tall trees and looking down on the right over the valley of the Jed Water to the Cheviot. The Jed Water winds for miles in serpentine bends below us, but apart from that the views from the highset road are splendid as we drive over slopes diversified by heather, bracken and gorse, passing close to the summit of Belling Hill (1,160 ft).

So we reach A68 after nearly five miles and turn right, crossing the Jed Water, which here flows through a wooded gorge, thereafter climbing into dense woodlands in which the beech trees are prominent. Once again one is struck by the vast difference between individual main roads, for this is a trunk road, one of the chief links between England and Scotland, yet it is rarely if ever crowded and utterly unspoilt.

After driving beside the fence of an extensive park we turn left for Hindhope, quickly climbing to open moors which are only broken by scattered clumps of forestry. Soon we pass the characteristic conical summits of Browndean Laws, both over 1,300 ft, features of almost every landscape in the country between the Cheviot and Carter Bar.

In the midst of the moors we reach a signposted junction where we go forward for Hownam, steering ever nearer to the summit of the Cheviot, and shortly descending steeply to cross the Kale Water, which winds through a bare and boggy high valley. At the next junction our way is left again for Hownam and subsequently left once more, avoiding a turn to Buchtrig. Now we follow the zigzag course of the Kale Water all the way to Hownam. There is dramatic though austere beauty in this valley though in bright weather the austerity is forgotten in the lovely contours of the smooth fells. Ultimately we bear left into the tiny but pretty village of Hownam, which has an unexpected row of eighteenth-century cottages, trim and well cared for.

Beyond it we continue above the Kale Water, then cross it but keep it closely on our right, where Hownam Law rises abruptly from the river's course to a height of 1,472 ft. At a signposted т-junction we take the Yetholm turn on the right, recrossing the Kale, and soon reach Town Yetholm, passing Romany House, a link with the traditional connection of Yetholm with the King of the Scottish gipsies, a fine Georgian mansion. The last official Romany Queen died in 1883 and was buried at Kirk Yetholm. Though nearly a century has passed since then Yetholm has changed very little. It is a pleasant little town or large village built round a green, with its sister village of Kirk Yetholm on the other bank of the Bowmont Water, to which we turn right at the end of the green and find that it, too, is partly built round a gracious green which gives it vastly added distinction.

A signpost on the right to Halterburn encourages the hardy to start the ascent of the Cheviot, for this is certainly one of the most popular starting places for the ascent. Our way is towards Wooler. We soon re-enter England at the sign of the Northumberland National Park and follow the valley of the Bowmont Water high above the river. As we drive through the village of

Kilham the views open out with hills apparently completely surrounding us. The Cheviot is probably seen in its most dramatic
light from this road though others claim that distinction for the
way along the upper Coquet. Even so, this is the only point
from which it is possible to make out the double rounded summit,
the highest point of which reaches 2,676 ft.

Westnewton is the next village we reach. Another path leads
from it to the Cheviot. After that Kirknewton with a towered
Gothic church is the only village we pass before reaching Wooler
by a well-signposted way and briefly along a major road. Wooler
is a pleasant Border town. When one has said that, one has said
almost all that can be said. Many use it as a centre for walking in
the Cheviot Hills, a few for motoring in the Border country, but
it is always quiet with remarkably little traffic passing through it.
We go straight through it, passing the handsome fountain
opposite the church then following the Newcastle road, A697,
and bearing right in this after crossing the Harthope burn. The
way is absolutely straightforward for about eight miles through
more gentle country, though the swelling ridges of the Cheviot
always enliven the views on our right.

As soon as we have crossed the Breamish river, however, we
turn right for Branton. The turning is signposted but a careful
watch is necessary to see it after our few miles of relatively swift
main road. In the village we bear left where the signpost reads
Glanton, continuing to a T-junction where we turn right for
Alnham, and right again at a subsequent junction for Great Ryle.
The next part of the route is a little complicated but shows a
quite different aspect of the Cheviot from what we have seen
before. At the next T-junction we turn right for Great Ryle,
going straight forward in this small settlement and soon reaching
Prendwick, then Alnham, which looks down into the valley of
the Aln, here a very small stream just starting its short course to
the sea.

At a junction at the foot of a hill beyond Alnham we bear
right for Netherton, shortly afterwards turning left for the latter,
and on reaching this remote village turn right for Harbottle and
Alwinton. Here the Cheviot remains on our right but the ridges
of Rothbury Forest are prominent on our left. The river Alwin
flows into the upper Coquet at Alwinton. Both are broad swift
streams. There is a lovely view of the two rivers as we approach

the village, and we can see the famous gorge of the Coquet in the distance where the hills seem to close in on the river valley and virtually encompass it. Finally we cross the Alwin and bear right into Alwinton, a very pretty village with a green which is traversed by the Alwinton burn.

Not so many years ago it was quite an adventure to drive to the road's end beyond Blindburn. Now a signpost in Alwinton clearly shows the way and the road is mainly well surfaced as it follows the course of the river, closely at most points but more distantly at others where it climbs into the moors to avoid the bogs of tributary streams. The scenery is always inspiring and when we reach Blindburn we are incontrovertibly in the massif of the Cheviot, even though the peak is far from the end of the road. However, it is less than two miles from Blindburn by path to the watershed which marks the boundary of England and Scotland at Beefstand Hill, which rises to 1,842 ft and commands views as magnificent as those from the Cheviot itself. I know of no place in the Borderland which has a distinction the equal of this, nor any ride to compare with the one from Alwinton to Blindburn.

We must return by the way we have come as far as Alwinton, where we take the Harbottle turn, soon crossing the Coquet and passing the fragmentary castle of Harbottle on a high mound. All the way downstream there is a magnificent contrast between the heathery moors, purple in late summer, and the green wooded slopes. At a fork we bear right for Holystone and Elsdon, and neglecting a turn to Holystone village go on for Hepple. So we reach a major road on the edge of Rothbury Forest and turn right for Otterburn. The rest is almost anticlimax but the scenery is always attractive. We climb over a bracken-covered ridge and continue over the moors to Elsdon, entering the village past the prominent green castle mound. Thence Otterburn is only just over three miles distant.

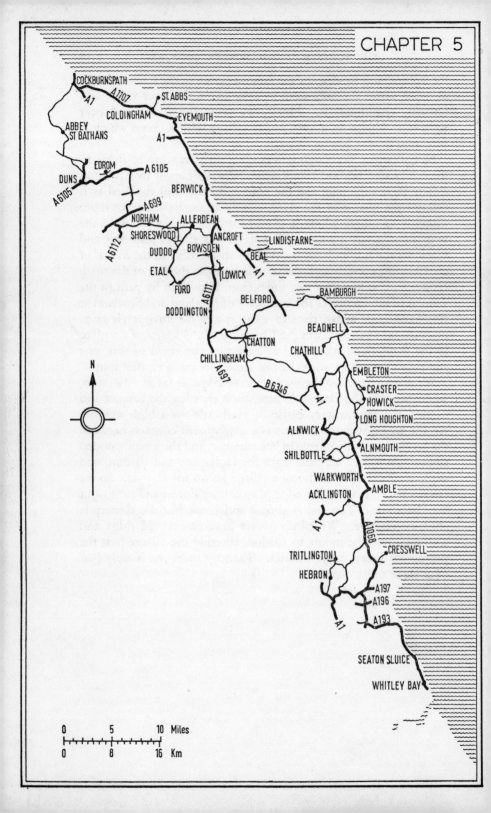

CHAPTER FIVE

COAST AND CASTLES

MOTORISTS who do not know the Northumberland coast are always amazed at its quietness, its lack of sophistication, its feeling of remoteness at every point to the north of the coalfields which reach from Newcastle as far as Ashington. It is a quietness and beauty which is continued beyond the Border without a break.

It is difficult to avoid superlatives when talking about this really lovely mixture of sandy beach, fishing village and low cliff. There is nothing quite like it in all England, while it is a graceful dispensation of providence never fully explained that the proximity of Tyneside and the coalfield has not led to its development to any measurable degree. It seems almost incredible that watering places like Alnmouth continue to exist and that fishing villages like Seahouses should scarcely have grown beyond their eighteenth- and nineteenth-century limits; that Bamburgh under the protection of its towering castle should live on in much the same shape and form as for hundreds of years. Yet these are facts which no one can gainsay.

In August there is a mild stir along the coast routes. In the hundreds of places where cars can be driven into the dunes on the very edge of the sandy beaches there are people. On fine summer Sundays the trek from Tyneside to the coast is to be avoided at all costs. At other times the byways are as quiet as the coastal byways of any part of England, the sands deserted for mile after mile, the sense of being away from it all so great as to approach a feeling of unreality.

This is a very historic as well as a spectacularly beautiful coast. The great castles of Bamburgh, Warkworth and the meagre but wonderfully imposing fragments of Dunstanburgh are all hard by the coast. Just inland Alnwick is one of the most historic homes in the country, the centrepiece of a town which has history round every corner. Even further south, within a quarter of a mile of Whitley Bay, which has become a far-flung suburb of Newcastle proudly retaining its own special rights, Seaton Delaval Hall, which is occasionally open to the public, is a magnificent house by Sir John Vanbrugh. Further north Holy Island and Berwick-upon-Tweed have an assured place in the historic annals of the country.

The first tour, one of the longest tours in the book, amounts to approximately 140 miles in total and is by way of being a master tour. It is not intended specifically for a single day, except perhaps for those who have only a day of their holiday in which to see this beautiful and storied part of England's heritage. It gives a byway route from Tyneside to Bamburgh and works south along the coast as far as the approach to Tynemouth, proving incidentally that it is possible to devise a route even through the coalfield which shows little trace of active industry. The ending is along the swift road from Tynemouth into Newcastle for those who live near this modern highway.

The outward byway route is enough for a single day, with a swift return by the Great North Road, which happily is rarely crowded. The coast between Bamburgh and Alnmouth has more than enough interest to last a full day with an easy return provided by the North Road, which is joined just on the Newcastle side of Alnwick. The rest of the tour, including Warkworth, will equally provide material for a full day. So three days is about the least time in which full justice can be done to it, while for people who are lucky enough to live within reach of all these places I hope the suggestions will provide matter for thought leading to many more days of happy motoring and sightseeing in the area.

From Tyneside the first stage inevitably is to Morpeth, either by A1 or by one of the byway routes which are not very much longer and have been described in previous chapters, particularly the way from Mitford into Newcastle in reverse. Mitford is less than two miles from Morpeth. That makes it unnecessary to travel over more than four miles of the Great North Road.

Morpeth, when we reach it, turns out to be a pleasant and old-looking town though in fact its historic legacy is less than that of many others. If we enter by the A1 we pass the castle which is not a castle, a strange but handsome castellated residence which houses the police force, cross the river Wansbeck and bear left

The river Coquet at Rothbury.   (Chapter 4.)

Rothley Crags, on the edge of Rothbury Forest.   (Chapter 4.)

The quiet expanse of Catcleugh reservoir.   (Chapter 4.)

The 'Beresford Arms', Whalton.   (Chapter 4.)

past a number of old timbered houses in the main shopping street and right within sight of the clock tower, which was originally a prison, in the market square. Nearby the town hall is said to have been designed by Sir John Vanbrugh at about the same time as Seaton Delaval but subsequent alterations, though they have not entirely destroyed Sir John's work, have very much modified it. The ruins of the ancient castle, which consist now of no more than an outer wall and fragments of a gatehouse, lie on the opposite side of the road to the modern police 'castle' and are extraordinarily difficult to find. I hope I shall not be described as an iconoclast if I say it is scarcely worth parking the car to make the expedition necessary to discover them.

Continuing on A1 by Newgate Street we soon reach the green fringe of the town and fork right in a narrow road for Fulbeck, which is well signposted but not always too easy to reach when south-bound traffic is heavy. We follow this pleasant byway, neglecting a right turn and reaching Hebron in about two miles. Here just short of the plain little church we turn right through the hamlet for Tritlington over the pleasant country of the coastal plain with an occasional glimpse of the sea far to our right. We pass the pele tower of Cockle Park quite close to the road, a particularly fine example with well preserved machicolation of these medieval homes of the Borderland.

We turn left into Tritlington at the next T-junction and bear right where the way is signposted Chevington, bearing left away from the Hall entrance and crossing a stream before bearing right at the next junction for Chevington again. Then at the next T-junction we turn right and at a crossroads left, continuing along the ensuing straight road towards Acklington but at a wider road bearing right for it. This sounds perhaps a little more complicated than it really is. The roads are well surfaced and signposted. It is only a matter of making certain that we choose the one we want.

At Acklington station and market, an unmistakable landmark, we turn left for Acklington Park, and left again for Guyzance in just over a quarter of a mile, with soon a distant view of Guyzance Hall through a gap in its surrounding woodlands. Soon our road enters hanging woods and crosses the river Coquet by a picturesque old mill. The ancient ruined chapel of St Wilfrid is on our right. On the further side of the bridge we bear left for Alnwick and just before a bridge over the wooded gorge of the Newton burn near the point where it joins the Coquet bear right for Hazon. This is one of the most distinguished parts of the whole ride, with its fine views of Coquetdale.

All too soon we veer away from this scene of natural beauty, crossing a low plateau and at a junction bear left for Shilbottle and Alnwick, continuing to both. The church of St James at Shilbottle is well worth seeing. It is basically a Norman building with a later but very impressive turreted tower, a far larger church than most in this part of the country, while the vicarage adjacent to the church incorporates part of the early vicarage pele tower. We continue past the church then turn left for Alnwick and follow the signposts to it by A1 past the comparatively modern Percy monument decorated with the Percy Lion on top and at the base, and enter the central square by the Hotspur Gate, one of the original fifteenth-century gates remarkably little altered.

There is so much to find and see in Alnwick that many people feel they are far from knowing it intimately after spending a whole day among its old stone buildings and historic memories. By far its most historic building is the castle, the gatehouse of which is passed on our road, though no possible justice is done to its manifold interest by such a cursory view. Happily it is open on most summer afternoons (but not Fridays and Saturdays) and shows all the features that one would expect of a sophisticated border fortress which served as one of the chief seats of the Percys from Norman times. A great deal of medieval work survives but even the exterior bears many traces of the nineteenth-century work of Salvin. However, the interior is elegant and the treasures it contains incomparable. Visitors are normally shown over the keep and armoury, the great chamber and library, as well as many of the principal apartments.

In the town itself the market place with its stone-paved streets is fascinating, with the eighteenth-century town hall its main feature apart from the fountain of similar date which is crowned by a carving of St Michael and the dragon. The old market cross has been replaced but the steps are probably medieval. The parish church of St Michael near the castle at the top of Bailiffgate is a fine fifteenth-century church in a singularly handsome position, while there is a wealth of fine Georgian houses here and

near the market place. Other features fairly easily found include
the eighteenth-century Brislaw Tower, but the gatehouse of the
Premonstratensian abbey and the fragments of Hulne Priory are
both well to the north of the town in the demesne of Hulne Park.

The entrance to the park, one of the most beautiful in Northumberland, is reached by the road opposite the castle entrance
which passes St Michael's church then bears left. Cars are
forbidden in the park (also bicycles and dogs) but it is the key to
some exceptionally lovely scenery on both banks of the river Aln,
grand wooded landscapes which are the equal of any park
landscapes in the north of England. The abbey gatehouse was
part of a Premonstratensian House founded in 1147. It is reasonably easy of access on the left bank of the Aln and quite near the
park entrance. The gatehouse is not contemporary with the
founding of the abbey but is a later medieval one restored in the
eighteenth century.

Hulne Friary, more commonly known as Hulne Priory, was
one of the earliest establishments of the Carmelites or White
Friars in England. It was founded probably towards the end of
the thirteenth century and dissolved with all the other monastic
establishments during the reign of Henry VIII. The ruins are
considerable and extremely interesting, though it is difficult
sometimes to distinguish between the original work and the
'improvements' made by the 1st Duke of Northumberland.
However, the plan of the monastic establishment is clear enough
and it is a really lovely walk of rather less than two miles from the
Alnwick entrance to its site.

Continuing by the Berwick road we cross the Lion bridge (the
lion is the Percy Lion which stands proudly on the parapet on
the centre of the bridge), and drive over the demesne, passing
the fragmentary ruin of the Chapel of St Leonard's Hospital on
our left and the base of the ancient Hefferlaw Tower.

There is no easy place to leave the main road until we have
driven about four miles, when we turn right for Bamburgh and
drive on through Chathill and at a T-junction towards North
Charlton. After that we turn right, again for Chathill, and thereafter follow the signposts to Chathill and Bamburgh. After
crossing a level crossing our road turns squarely left but beyond
a belt of woodland we leave the direct Bamburgh road and bear
left for Newham over a railway bridge, going forward at a

subsequent crossroads for Newham Hall, and at the next
T-junction in about a mile turn right. Then at a fork by a farmhouse opposite a spinney on a mound we bear left and after that
again go straight on for Bamburgh, soon catching our first glimpse
of the castle across the fields before turning right in B1341 for the
last mile. It looks from here as if Bamburgh were all castle, so
completely does it dominate the little town.

We reach Bamburgh by the lovely tree-shaded green with its
picturesque stone well. Before looking at the castle the logical
thing to do is to bear left at the green to the Grace Darling
museum and the remarkably beautiful tomb of this famous lady in
the churchyard, while the church itself is a magnificent and
elaborate one. Grace Horsley Darling was born 24 November
1815 and died 20 October 1842 at the age of 26. Many people
regard the Grace Darling story as a legend but it is sober fact.
Grace took part with her father, who was keeper of the Long-
stone Lighthouse, in the rescue of survivors from the *Forfarshire*.
Her bravery was universally recognized and made an equally
universal appeal. She is buried in the churchyard a little to the
south of the memorial tomb but the original effigy is in the
church, where it was placed for safety after a storm in 1885,
when the canopy was blown down. It is said that the position of
the memorial was chosen so as to be visible to passing seafarers.
Certainly there is a grand view of the sea from this part of the
churchyard.

The singularly lovely church is dedicated to St Aidan, who
died here in 651 when, as the Venerable Bede records, there was
a church of timber with an active congregation. Both the original
Saxon church and the Norman one which succeeded it have been
swept away, but there is compensation in the spaciousness of the
Early English architecture of the nave and chancel and in the still
later fourteenth-century transepts. It is only a few hundred yards
from the church to the castle, which looks medieval in every
respect. In fact only the exceptionally fine keep is Norman, the
remainder having been built or rebuilt in castle form during the
last 150 years. Two features of special interest are the rock
outcrop, the Whin Sill, on which the castle is built and the little
shrine with cross which has been cut in the rock under the castle
walls. The castle is open to visitors every afternoon.

Now we go forward close beside the sand dunes for Seahouses, and soon have a fine view through a gap in the dunes to the Farne Islands and their lighthouses. A short climb to the summit of the dunes will reveal Holy Island and the incomparable group of buildings which have a silhouette different from any other place in England. There are, too, magnificent sandy beaches near the road before we reach Seahouses. The main road by-passes this ancient fishing village, but for interest it is worth turning left down the steep hill leading to the harbour which is picturesque and colourful. There is an equally picturesque fishing village immediately behind the harbour, an ancient village of narrow streets and little squares. To reach these we go on as far as we can from the end of the fishing harbour, then turn right and weave our way through the old town before turning left to resume the coast road, which is now very near the sea. It is amazing how many people frequently pass Seahouses without really appreciating its beauty and interest.

Soon we are beside the dunes again and there is another well worthwhile detour at Beadnell to the harbour, to which the road is marked 'No through road'. Soon there is an alternative road on the right which leads to a car park adjacent to the beach but for a brief glimpse it is better to go straight on. There is no real difficulty in turning at the harbour, which lies only a hundred yards beyond the entrance to the 'No through road'. This is another colourful scene, not really a harbour but a safe anchorage for yachts, with eighteenth-century lime kilns on the low cliff which bounds the sands.

Returning to the main road we continue for Newcastle, now bearing away from the sea. From this point onwards we shall be frequently encouraged to drive straight on to Newcastle, most of the roads indicated leading ultimately to the Great North Road, at Alnwick or Morpeth. These are quick ways back to the Tyne-side metropolis but can be regarded only as routes to be taken if time is short, leaving the rest of the tour for another day. None of these direct roads could conceivably be called beautiful.

Here at Beadnell we pass the church which is distinguished by a curious tower and short spire. Just beyond it we turn left, then right in a few yards, so returning to the Alnwick road, in which we turn left. At the first crossroads our way is towards Embleton, as if we were making directly for Newcastle. This is a pretty road and still has the feel of the sea, which is often visible even though we are now considerably further from it. We pass a signpost to Newton-by-the-Sea (a good beach and a few bungalows and cottages) and after that catch our first glimpse of Dunstanburgh Castle high on its headland.

Soon we enter Embleton, an interesting village with a fine vicarage tower house or pele which, curiously, was built at the expense of Merton College, Oxford, to which its living was granted. Opposite the church and vicarage we take the turning for Craster and there bear right where the signpost reads Dunstanburgh, continuing to the furthest point we can go by car. This is a full mile from the actual ruin, though the distant view is fine and cannot well be improved upon by going nearer. The castle is a fourteenth-century stronghold, one of those held by John of Gaunt. It is certainly worth a visit by people to whom a 2-mile walk over fields is no more than an aperitif to more strenuous things.

Returning briefly on our way, we now make for Craster, turning left in just over a mile, with another good view to Dunstanburgh Castle. We pass yet another ruined pele on our right as we approach the village, which is a jolly little seaside village with a small harbour and is the key to a magnificent cliff path going southward, as well to another route to Dunstanburgh to the north.

Howick is our next objective. It is reached by returning a short distance by the way we have come, then turning left, passing under a ruined stone gateway which spans the road and bearing left again for Howick at the end of the fine estate of Howick Hall. Now we are following the coastline closely again but at Howick we go forward for Longhoughton (the gardens of Howick Hall, incidentally, are open daily on summer afternoons and there is an ingenious shilling-in-the-slot meter, a strange contrast with the procedure at most historic homes).

At Longhoughton after passing the square-towered church we turn left for Boulmer, passing a small R.A.F. base, and bearing right in the fishing village where the way is signposted Lesbury. Here there is another series of good beaches. Half a mile short of Lesbury, which is seen in the distance, we turn left for Alnmouth and drive into the compact shopping centre of this most pleasant place which has a splendid sandy beach. Alnmouth is what used to be called a watering place. It is still very much in the shape of a late Victorian holiday resort with positively no modern development—quiet, reserved, charming, a perfect place in which to spend a quiet holiday with not a single discordant note and extraordinarily little feeling of the twentieth century.

We leave Alnmouth by the Newcastle road, shortly crossing the Aln, and at a roundabout turn left on A1068 for Ashington, keeping parallel with the Aln, across which there is the finest of all views of Alnmouth. Soon we reach Warkworth, with a fine view of the castle as we approach it over the new bridge which bypasses the ancient bridge and gate which, however, are both standing and add real distinction to the scene.

Warkworth Castle is a very distinguished ruin. Its earliest part dates from the twelfth century, much of it from the succeeding century, though the keep is a fifteenth-century building for which the Percys, Earls of Northumberland, were responsible. One of the sights of Warkworth is the Hermitage, a chapel cut out of the solid rock on the bank of the river with bare living-rooms adjoining it, and probably dating from the fourteenth century. The only method of access is by the boats which ply from the riverside just below the castle, a most interesting expedition and a reliable one, too, since the Hermitage, as well as the castle, is in the care of the Ministry of Works and the boats are quite regular during the summer months. Before reaching the castle our way is through the market place, past the medieval market cross and up the steep main street. Then we go on for Amble beside the wide waterway of the Coquet, and in Amble follow the Newcastle signposts.

So far on this tour there has been scarcely a sign of industry since we left Newcastle, none since we left Morpeth. Now it is a little more difficult to avoid commercial landscapes; it is a matter of avoiding—as far as possible—the collieries and the areas which have been more or less spoilt by twentieth-century development. You might well judge after half an hour's driving that it is not so bad as you feared, for there is still a great deal of green and open countryside.

Continuing for a time towards Ashington, we pass an opencast mining site now being regenerated, then at the roundabout by the 'Widdrington' inn we bear left for Druridge along a tree-lined road which quickly brings us back to the coast and takes us through Cresswell, later running along the summit of a low cliff towards Lynemouth. We cross the river Lyne by a road which we share with a colliery railway and take the first turning on the left, which is signposted Ashington and Newbiggin, going straight on again shortly, and beyond a disused windmill go forward on A197.

After going under a railway bridge, however, our way is sharp left across pleasant fields to B1334, where we turn right and continue on this road until we join an A road to cross a level crossing and the Wansbeck, here widening towards its estuary. And so into Bedlingtonshire (it is pleasant to see the old territorial name revived), turning left on B1330 for Bedlington station. Continuing towards Blyth, we cross the handsome new bridge over the Blyth river for Bebside and on reaching A193 turn right away from Blyth towards Newcastle. In a quarter of a mile, however, beyond a level crossing we turn left by a garage in a currently unsignposted road which is still largely rural and brings us to another main road, in which we turn left towards North Shields, but at the next crossroads turn left on B1327 temporarily towards Blyth.

It is a fine stretch of unspoilt country which lies between us and the distantly seen Blyth. At a T-junction on its outskirts we turn right on the way signposted quite simply Beach, shortly reaching the seashore and turning right in the main coast road, which is all too often a double carriageway, though rarely congested. The ride from here to Whitley Bay has parking places galore, as well as many refreshment kiosks and the other amenities of a popular coast road. At Seaton Sluice a road on the right leads shortly and rather unexpectedly to the magnificent mansion (open to the public on summer Sundays and Wednesdays as well as occasionally at other times) of Seaton Delaval Hall, which is often described as the masterpiece of Sir John Vanbrugh, the architect of Blenheim Palace and many other of Britain's most magnificent homes.

Just beyond Seaton Sluice we bear left to the sea front and cliffs of Whitley Bay and end this exciting and varied tour along a road which is a genuine coast road but little known except to residents, perhaps because most people think it is too near to Tyneside to be worth a second thought in terms of beauty. Far from it. The cliffs are really superb, the coastal scenery always attractive. At the approach to Tynemouth, rather than wend our way by the old main road, we turn right on A1058 within sight of Tynemouth's golden sands. If our destination is central Newcastle that is a singularly painless way of reaching it and brings us into its outskirts by the southern end of the Town Moor.

Our next tour, a relatively short one, is best undertaken from Bamburgh or Seahouses, or from Alnwick, though clearly it is perfectly feasible for a long day's tour from Newcastle, all roads joining at Belford. It includes some of the finest scenery between the sea and the Cheviot, a remarkably little known area where even the main roads carry light traffic and the byways practically none.

If we are starting from Bamburgh we follow B1342 as far as Belford, a good road by any reckoning with magnificent views of Budle Bay at intervals along it. On reaching the Great North Road we turn right into Belford village, an extremely attractive one with a market cross, not a medieval one, several fine Georgian houses, and a church which was originally Norman and retains its Norman chancel arch with zigzag moulding on the east side. Belford's heyday may have been in coaching days but it is still a very gracious place and apparently a prosperous one.

Just short of the market cross we turn left in West Street, which is signposted Wooler, past the stylish war memorial hall on the right, built in the style of Georgian halls. We quickly reach open country, bearing left at the first junction which is signposted Wooler. This is a hawthorn-hedged road where the hedges do not preclude a view of the countryside and there is an unhampered prospect from the top of the first ridge along the Till valley on our right and forward to the Cheviot. Shortly afterwards we pass a dense conifer wood and turn right, again for Wooler, soon crossing the wide Till by a fine stone bridge. And so into Chatton village, at the end of which we turn left for Chillingham.

Chillingham is best known for its herd of pure white cattle which graze in the park of the castle. The entrance to the park is by a turning on the left opposite the post office. This road takes us down past the church, another originally Norman building with many good features, especially the south doorway. The most striking part of the interior is the Grey altar tomb, a monument to Sir Ralph Grey, who died in 1443, and his wife Elizabeth. It is a really lovely work of art. One hundred and fifty yards beyond the church one can obtain the services of a guide for a modest fee to show the Chillingham herd, an opportunity which on no account should be missed. The castle, unhappily not open to the public at present, is largely a fourteenth-century building and according to most authorities one of the finest medieval castles in the county, finer perhaps even than Alnwick itself.

We return to the main road and, going forward, follow the park wall, passing impressive lodge gates, thereafter bearing left, and continuing along the edge of the park. Next we have a truly wild and rugged ride, climbing to the summit of the moor past many rock outcrops, in contrast with the gracious park lands of Chillingham, the wall of which climbs improbably to the very summit of the moor on our left after we turn away from it. Beyond that our way is over bare heather-covered slopes. As we begin to descend there is some pastureland and occasional fields of oats intended for winter feeding stuff and the beginnings of considerable forestry. But for the most part the landscape is bare and there are few farms.

After several miles of this lonely but always interesting driving we reach the A1 at North Charlton and turn right in it for just over a mile, then right again on B6347 for Eglingham and South Charlton, soon coming to the latter and continuing straight through it. On reaching B6346 we turn right, still for Eglingham, and at this point are joined by readers who start at Alnwick by the way alongside Hulne Park. In Eglingham we go through the large and pleasant village for Wooler, soon passing under a green tunnel of trees, later emerging at a viewpoint which commands the full beauty of the Cheviot range across the wide Breamish valley. At the next signpost we go straight on for Chillingham but just beyond a little hamlet fork left for East Lilburn, crossing the Breamish by a picturesque one-arched stone bridge and bearing right at the next junction.

One might be forgiven if one passed through East Lilburn without recognizing it, for it is small and lacks any major feature. We go forward in it, then bear right for Ilderton beside the school, turning right across the Lilburn stream by another picturesque stone bridge, and bearing right at a subsequent junction which is signposted Chillingham. In less than a mile we leave the Chillingham road for a turning on the left signposted Broomhouse, bearing left at the first junction, and crossing a subsequent crossroads, where our way is signposted Wooler. Soon we descend into the Till valley, where there is another outstanding view of the Cheviot range. Our road bears left down to the river, which we ultimately cross by yet another ancient high-arched bridge as we turn away from the Wooler road for Doddington and subsequently turn left again for Doddington following the lower slopes of Dod Law on a shelf high above the valley.

We continue to a major road where our way is right towards Berwick, soon passing through Doddington and at the end of the village turning left for Nesbit, past the ruined gabled tower house or pele, one of the latest to be constructed before the union between England and Scotland and now partially obscured by trees. Opposite this we turn right, and right at the next junction after about two miles by a farm group, but left at the next two junctions, then right for Ford.

It is worth turning right (our direct way is to the left) in Ford to see the model village, the castle and the church. The castle, now one of the premises of the Northumberland Education Committee, is mostly modern but there are two old towers. The church has a most interesting bell turret, which is probably contemporary with the earliest work in the church, which dates from the thirteenth century. The village is very Victorian but remarkably successful, a model village in every sense of the term and a strange settlement indeed to find in the midst of the open country.

After seeing Ford we go on as for Berwick through Etal, another interesting village lying off the road with a substantial fragment of its castle, including the south-east entrance tower which probably dates from the fourteenth century. Many of the cottages have been re-roofed but some survivals of an older village are still thatched and make a pleasant contrast with the usual appearance of Northumberland villages.

Returning from the castle to the main road, we continue to Duddo, which also boasts the fragment of a castle, the ruined tower of which is in a commanding position on a high rock outcrop seen far and wide over the countryside. Just beyond it we bear left at the T-junction for Tiptoe. Duddo Stones, a famous megalithic monument of five massive stones, can be discerned half a mile to our right on high ground. They can be reached on

foot but it is a long walk across fields with no clear path. At the
next crossroads we bear right for Norham and follow the signposts to it, crossing a major road where the signpost reads
Norham Station.

And so into Norham, a lovely village, which has a very fine
thirteenth-century cross, a cluster of pillars with a conical top,
set on high steps, and the green is surrounded by pleasant houses
of many periods. There is, incidentally, a fine prospect from the
village green of the high-set castle, while the church, dedicated to
St Cuthbert, has a Norman chancel and chancel arch, and the
pillars on the south side of the nave are unmistakably Norman.
The way to the castle is obvious by a road close to the bank of
the Tweed, which here divides England from Scotland and is a
broad swift-flowing moat, as every river dividing one country
from another should be. The castle in the Middle Ages was a
possession of the Bishops of Durham and was counted one of the
strongest of all border castles. Its pride is the Norman keep
built about 1160, and its history includes several sieges by the
Scots, who were never successful in reducing it to ruins or
making it inoperative in the scheme of English border defence.

We continue past the castle to the first road junction, where
we turn right (unsignposted) along a very straight road which
takes us to a T-junction in just over half a mile. There we turn
left, soon crossing the Berwick-Cornhill road for Ancroft, later
crossing a major road at Allerdean and bearing left at a subsequent
unsignposted T-junction. At Ancroft we bear right in a major
road which is signposted Lowick, continuing through the
village and bearing left a little way beyond it for Haggerston.
At the next T-junction we turn right, once more for Lowick.
After that we neglect a left turn to Haggerston and a right one to
Berrington but turn left at the next T-junction, soon crossing a
little stream, the course of which we follow (in a deep combe on
our right). At the next T-junction our way is to the right to
Lowick and in a few yards right again. We cross the next major
road for Alnwick, still driving through a most exciting and
colourful landscape, now passing high rocks, now an extensive
conifer forest with open moors on our left.

At a T-junction we turn left for Belford, climbing over Belford
Moor, with a glimpse of Holy Island and its buildings from the
summit before descending into Belford and rejoining our

outward way. If we are making for Bamburgh we turn right at
Belford cross and take the first on the left, if for Alnwick we turn
right down the Great North Road. Either way is a quiet and
pleasant ending to a tour which has a great deal of historic
interest as well as scenic beauty in every mile.

The last tour in this chapter takes us along the coast for
several miles on either side of the Border and in addition through
some charming country just to the east of the coastline round
Abbey St Bathans. It is fairly straightforward and its 110 miles
are just about right for a long leisurely day's touring. Berwick is
by far the best centre for this part of the Border country but it is
obvious that the tour could be completed successfully from
Bamburgh or the seaside resorts further south, or from some of
the Scottish coastal towns such as Dunbar.

For those who seek the atmosphere of the Border, however,
Berwick is a must, a town to be explored at leisure and an easy
town in which to obtain accommodation to suit most purses. Its
chief interest, of course, is that it is the Border town of Border
towns which for hundreds of years was sometimes Scottish,
sometimes English. Today it is firmly within the realm of
England, though it is an interesting fact that most of its citizens
speak with a Scottish accent. Historically it is a free town,
neither English nor Scottish, its so-called liberties extending
about three miles north of the Tweed, a county in its own right.

Historians have virtually lost count of the number of times
which Berwick changed hands. The most reliable estimate places
the number at thirteen between the twelfth century and the end of
the fifteenth century. An army of Edward IV captured it in
1482 for England and the Scots never again penetrated its defences.
The walls were built originally in the reign of Edward I in
association with the castle, of which there is now no trace. The
Edwardian walls were completely reconstructed in Elizabethan
times, though it is possible that some small fragments remain of
the earlier fortifications. The Elizabethan walls, however, are of
enormous interest and are said to be the work of the French
engineer Vauban. They closely followed the plan of the walls of
Antwerp and made Berwick-upon-Tweed the most up-to-date
town in Britain, at least as regards its defences. The wall walk,
which almost encircles the town, is of special interest and
incidentally gives a very fine view of many of the town's historic

buildings. The 2nd Earl of Bedford was the first governor and commander-in-chief of the newly fortified town. His presence gave an importance to the new Berwick which in a sense it has never lost. The fortifications did not come under attack for the Scots must have realized that they were virtually impregnable.

That is only the beginning of Berwick's interest. The view up river from the road bridge to the railway bridge is one of the finest of its kind in England. The fifteen-arched seventeenth-century Berwick bridge itself is a magnificent feat of engineering beside which the modern ferro-concrete bridge appears positively out of character. Then there is the parish church of the Holy Trinity which was pulled down and rebuilt about 1650 during the Commonwealth, when Colonel Fenwicke was governor, a period when extraordinarily few churches were being built in England. Many people, however, mistake the town hall for the parish church, a quite understandable mistake, since the town hall, which was built in the middle of the eighteenth century, has a fine tower and spire and the bells in the tower serve as the bells of the parish church.

We leave Berwick by A1, signposted Edinburgh, a fine cliff road and by far the best scenic road in the district for all that it is a main highway. However, motorists who are accustomed to the A1 further south will have a pleasant surprise at the relative lack of traffic in this sector. We soon leave it for a right fork, A1107, signposted Eyemouth, with a distant view of St Abb's Head almost immediately.

On reaching Eyemouth we turn right over the Eye bridge towards the town centre. It is a short detour to the harbour but one well worth making, for Eyemouth is very much a fishing port and it is not unusual for the fishing boats to be tied up at the quay or in the early morning for a fish market to be in progress. If we go on beyond the quay we shall come to a point adjacent to Eyemouth's fine sandy beach. There can be few seaside towns which combine so admirably the character of a small holiday resort with that of an active fishing town.

We leave Eyemouth by the Coldingham road, another high cliff road which commands splendid views to St Abb's Head, and in Coldingham bear right for St Abb's. Coldingham has one interesting link with the past, the parish church. This is in fact the choir of a medieval monastery, though much restored and partly rebuilt. There are fragments of the monastic buildings beside it, on the site of an early foundation of St Ebba. The market cross is just to our left before we turn right for St Abb's.

St Abb's is interesting in a very different way, a fishing village now, as it has been for hundreds of years, perched on a cliff above the harbour, commanding a splendid seascape, especially round the bay which ends at St Abb's Head, where a number of detached rocks break up the waters of the bay.

From here we must return to Coldingham, which we leave now by the Dunbar road, following this quiet highway for several miles. It is a very pretty road, wooded at first in contrast with the open cliff scenery and later commanding unrestricted views towards the Lammermuir Hills as we drive forward over Coldingham Moor, parts of which have been afforested though still it is mainly a summer grazing ground for sheep. Soon we begin to descend from the 700-ft level of the moor and hundreds of square miles of the plain which bounds the Firth of Forth come into view. Later in the immediate foreground lovely Pease Bay with its encircling girdle of red rocks comes into view. Just short of a deep wooded combe we take an obscure unsignposted road down to it. This road bends back from our way, then bears left sharply downhill and crosses a ford just short of the beach before climbing the steep hill on the other side.

On rejoining the main road near Cove station we turn left into Cockburnspath, beyond which we bear right for Abbey St Bathans, enjoying some distinguished long sea views as we climb into the foothills of the Lammermuir. We soon reach the moors and after several miles turn squarely right, once more following the signposts for Abbey St Bathans, and continuing to this remote little village which is set in a splendid wooded valley watered by the Whiteadder. The village takes its name from the abbey which was an important one in the Middle Ages. Its church incorporates part of the fabric of the abbey church and contains the tomb of a prioress—a singularly beautiful piece of sculpture. We cross the Whiteadder before passing the church, then climb high above the valley of the river which here runs in a deep and densely wooded glen, ultimately emerging once more on the moors.

It is a steep descent through dense woods to a major road, in which we turn left for Duns, continuing for Duns at the next

junction and ultimately joining the main road. Duns is the county
town of Berwickshire, but a notably quiet and retiring county
town. It has nothing that is remotely medieval, because it was
not founded until 1588, when the former Duns higher up the
Law had been utterly destroyed during an English raid. One of
the oldest buildings is the church but even that was not founded
until the last years of the eighteenth century. Even so, Duns
retains a number of eighteenth- and nineteenth-century houses
and has a spacious market square which gives the impression of
greater age than it can strictly claim.

We leave Duns by the Berwick road (Murray Street on the left
of the market square) but after nearly a mile where the Berwick
road turns squarely right go straight on, bearing left at a park
gate and lodge, and following the park wall through a tunnel of
trees, soon passing Buxley manor farm. This is slightly complicated. If we have come the right way, avoiding two unsignposted
left forks, we should reach Edrom village, in which we turn left,
taking the 'No through road' for a short detour to the church.

Edrom church itself is modern but nearby is a little stone
mausoleum with a fine Norman doorway rich in moulding on
the arch and capitals, a part of the original parish church and well
worth seeing. We return to the post office at the crossroads,
going forward over them past a telephone box (i.e. if we do not
visit the church we turn right at the crossroads). So we quickly
reach a major road in which we turn left but after about 200 yards
veer right opposite a war memorial down a fine beech avenue,
continuing for about one and a half miles until we cross the
Blackadder Water. At a subsequent T-junction we turn left and
on reaching a major road left again but leave this major road in a
quarter of a mile for a minor one on the right signposted Whit-
some, bearing right on the outskirts of the latter village for
Coldstream and Ladykirk, and soon crossing a major road for
the same destination.

The hills now are far behind us but the country is pleasant
farming country and though level is never monotonous as we
draw near the mighty Tweed. At the next crossroads our way is
to the left where the signpost reads Norham. Thereafter we
keep to the wider road as far as the Ladykirk turn, where we
leave the main road and turn left beside a fountain to the interesting church which was begun in 1500 and endowed by King

Shepherd and sheep on The Cheviot, near Catcleugh reservoir.   (Chapter 4.)

College burn, near Westnewton, and beyond, the misty Cheviot.   (Chapter 4.)

Norman doorway of
Lindisfarne priory on
Holy Island.
(Chapter 5.)

The well-restored
Bamburgh Castle,
impressive on the
basalt rock of the
Whin Sill.
(Chapter 5.)

James IV to commemorate his escape from drowning in the
Tweed. The fabric is an unusual but attractive example of the
Tudor Gothic style.

Returning from the church to the major road, we turn left in it
by the fountain where the signpost reads Norham, soon crossing
a fine stone bridge over the Tweed into England. In Norham
we bear right for Cornhill, continuing as far as Shoreswood and
crossing a major road by the 'Salutation' inn, where our way is
signposted Allerdean. After about two and a half miles we turn
right at another crossroads by West Allerdean Methodist church
for Duddo, driving pleasantly but without excitement along this
road for just over two miles. Then we turn left at a crossroads
just beyond the church and go forward in a major road, following
this to the left (signposted Bowsden) and continuing along it as
far as Bowsden, neglecting a left fork after a quarter of a mile.
Just beyond Bowsden we reach another major road in which we
turn right for a quarter of a mile and left into an unsignposted
lane. After a short half mile we must look for an obscure turning
on the right which is also unsignposted, a one-track road between
hedges which, apart from one or two small twists of recent
origin, especially where it takes us over streams, follows precisely
the course of a Roman road for several miles and crosses a crossroads in Lowick village.

Soon Belford Moor looms up on our left and about three miles
beyond Lowick, at a crossroads, we turn left for Hetton Law,
where the Roman road goes on ahead of us as straight as a die.
Neglecting a right turn at a T-junction (this would take us to
Hetton Hall) we turn right for Chatton at a signposted T-junction
and left for Belford in a quarter of a mile. This way takes us over
the lovely Belford Moor, which commands views in every
direction but most memorably forward to Holy Island and the
coast between Berwick and Bamburgh.

When we reach Belford we turn left in the Great North Road,
running parallel with the sea, of which there are many charming
views, and positively enjoy these 7 miles of easy motoring after
the rather difficult byway route we have followed for the last 20.
The turn for Holy Island is clearly signposted near the 'Plough'
hotel. A lesser signpost reads Lindisfarne Priory. It is about two
miles from the high road to the beginning of the causeway which
links the mainland with the island. As this is one of the high-

B.C.—6

lights of the tour it is essential to discover in advance when it is possible to drive over the causeway, which at low tide gives no trouble at all but for nearly six hours in the day is quite impassable. It is amazing how many people arrive apparently without any idea of the state of the tides.

There is an atmosphere about Holy Island shared by no other sacred site in England. In a sense it was the cradle of Christianity in this country, and the ruins of Lindisfarne Priory are the mecca of thousands of pilgrims every year. In fact Lindisfarne represented the Celtic Christianity which spread from Ireland to Iona, and from Iona to other parts of Scotland and the north of England. Even so, it was founded in 635, a generation or more after St Augustine landed in Kent but long before any other Christian settlement had been made in the far north. It was the see of a bishopric from then until its destruction during a Danish raid towards the end of the ninth century. But it was always recognized as a famous centre of early Christian worship and was refounded as a dependency of the monastery of Durham less than twenty years after the Norman Conquest. It continued a useful life until the Dissolution and substantial ruins of the medieval priory remain. Their interest is secondary to that of the site itself, though the red sandstone gives a picturesque quality which makes them among the most attractive in the Border country.

The rest of the tour is inevitably anticlimax. We return by the causeway through Beal to the Great North Road and turn right in it to Berwick, passing the park of Haggerston Castle, now sardonically a caravan centre, although set in wonderfully pleasant surroundings. There are, too, a few glimpses of the sea but little of real interest until we approach the Tweed and drive over the bridge back to our starting point.

THE LOWER TWEED AND LAMMERMUIR HILLS

THERE IS A WEALTH of historic and scenic interest within a few miles of the Border on the Scottish side. In many ways it is a more friendly country than the stern Northumbrian uplands, yet it belongs to the same tradition. It has precisely the same history of constant border raids stretching over nearly 500 years and in Scotland there are legends galore of English atrocities, just as in Northumberland there are traditions of Scottish brutality and the constant raids which took place during these troubled centuries.

The border country on the Scottish side is very beautiful, with hills rising to heather-covered moorlands from the Tweed, perhaps the finest heather moorlands in Scotland, certainly as magnificent as any in the central or northern highlands to which so many go to see the heather in August and early September.

The tours described in this chapter include one which takes us up and over the Lammermuir, one which is confined to the historic places of the Tweed valley to which Sir Walter Scott has contributed so much that has proved permanent, and another which skirts the hills rising to the north-west of it. All are lovely tours but the first has a special distinction, if only because of the two routes we follow over the Lammermuir which reveal this gorgeous country in all its colour and all its scenic distinction. Even on a dull day when the hilltops are covered in mist there is beauty in every mile. On a fine day when the sun picks out the valleys and the hilltops there is scarcely anything in Great Britain to surpass it, and that in spite of the inevitable works which have been carried out in the Lammermuir Hills to construct a reservoir and have changed the surrounding scenery out of all recognition. But not necessarily for the worse, for there is beauty in this man-made harnessing of nature and little or nothing remains of the gashes made by digging lake beds and constructing new roads a few years after the deed is done.

CHAPTER 6

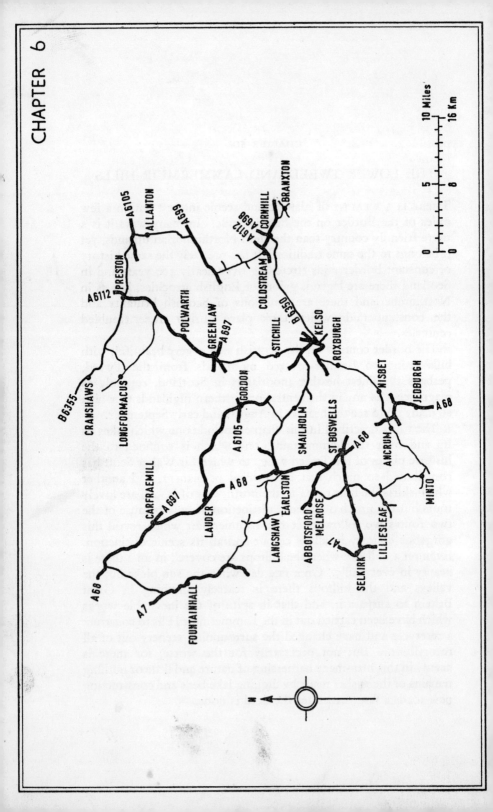

Convenient centres are relatively few and far between. Kelso is probably the best because it commands all the routes described in this chapter, not only those of the first tour. Peebles is another better-known resort from which access is relatively easy. It is possible to drive from Berwick, or even from Selkirk or Jedburgh. In any case Kelso is our starting place, and an extremely interesting one, which must be explored before we start the tour. Sir Walter Scott described Kelso as the most beautiful village in Scotland. Sober fact demands the correction that it is a town in every sense of the term and, though it retains Scott's beauty, is very much a business and commercial burgh. It was formerly a great centre of border warfare, and two of its most famous events were the crowning of James III in 1460 and the proclamation of King James VIII in 1715. Its chief link with the Middle Ages is the abbey, one of the finest in southern Scotland, a ruin which has many Norman and Early English features. It was founded early in the twelfth century by King David I and after the Reformation came into the hands of the Dukes of Roxburghe, who presented it as a public monument in 1919. For about 100 years in the seventeenth and eighteenth centuries the transept was used as a parish church. Many people are puzzled by the cloister, which at first glance appears Norman since it is in the Romanesque style, but it is a memorial to the 8th Duke of Roxburghe and his Duchess, who died early in the present century. Altogether, however, the ruins make a surprisingly handsome contribution to a town which otherwise is distinguished in almost every building, especially those surrounding the fine square, the most prominent of which is the towered Court House, though there are a great number of pleasant Georgian houses and hotels. The bridge over the Tweed is by Rennie, the architect of London Bridge, and a very fine bridge it is, with a splendid and indeed the only practical view for casual wayfarers of Floors Castle, the seat of the Dukes of Roxburghe which was designed by Sir John Vanbrugh in 1718, but completely reconstructed in the Tudor style towards the middle of the nineteenth century.

We leave Kelso for this 90 mile scenic tour by Roxburgh Street, A6089, keeping close by the wide waterway of the Tweed and passing an imposing entrance to Floors Castle. At the end of the park wall we fork right for Greenlaw on B6364, an exceedingly pleasant country road. In England it would be called a byway.

It crosses the Eden Water by the park of Newton Don, passes through Stichill by the pretentious entrance to Stichill House, and soon comes within sight of the late-eighteenth-century sham ruin of Hume Castle, which does not deserve to be dismissed with as much contempt as it usually receives, for it is a reconstruction of a thirteenth-century fortress of the Humes and preserves some of the earthworks of the original fortress. Just beyond it we turn right, where there is a long view across the Tweed valley to the Cheviot past the unusual cairn war memorial of Hume. The long, strangely even line of the Lammermuir fills the whole horizon ahead of us.

We join a main road to enter Greenlaw, a compact little town and one of the most picturesque in this part of Scotland, bearing right into the town over the Blackadder Water to the central square, which is built round a green, a large part of which is taken up by the handsome domed classical town hall. The tall tower of the church nearby dates from the eighteenth century. Indeed, there is a wholly classical air about Greenlaw, which we leave by the Duns road on the left of the green, then cross the heather-covered Greenlaw Moor, passing through the village of Polwarth to within a mile of Duns. As we have already explored Duns, there is no need to enter it on this occasion. Instead we turn left where the signpost reads Duns Golf Course and another, less conspicuous, Longformacus, steering into the heart of the Lammermuir country along a lovely tree-lined road. As we ascend to the moors there is an exceptional view to the left with the Eildon Hills an unmistakable feature, as they often are of landscapes of the Tweed valley.

Soon we approach Longformacus, a village thrust further than any other into the Lammermuir, not particularly memorable but a pleasant group of cottages by a tree-fringed stream. Here we go forward for Gifford, bearing right after crossing Dye Water and soon rising on to the high moors and quickly reaching a height of more than 1,300 ft with a breathtaking view on the right into the valley of the Whiteadder. It is a grand ride over the moors at any season of the year but especially in late summer and early autumn, when the moors are quite literally alive with colour, the purple of the heather setting off the green of the bracken. So luxurious is the heather that many farmers bring their beehives into the hills for the whole season. If you stop it is quite likely that the air will be filled with the hum of bees though it is said that there are not so many as there were a few years ago.

Soon we cross a tributary stream of the Whiteadder, then climb steadily, going forward when we join another road coming in on our right and ultimately crossing the watershed, so that our view is northward to the Firth of Forth before we begin the steep descent, in some ways the most dramatic part of the whole route. We fall off the hills and at the first crossroads turn right for Garvald, a very charming road which leads through several woods, negotiating a steep hairpin bend, and brings us into Garvald, where we bear right over an old stone bridge for Nunraw, soon passing the entrance to the modern Sancta Maria Abbey, and at the top of the hill passing a large farm which incorporates a pele tower.

Now we are reapproaching the Lammermuir Hills in the opposite direction from which we have just crossed them, and entirely different they look. As soon as we have crossed the ridge we begin to descend the valley of the Whiteadder on a shelf high above the twisting silver coils of the river, later riding high above the new Whiteadder reservoir. Continuing down the valley, we keep to B6355 where a turn to the left is signposted Dunbar, soon crossing the Whiteadder and passing through Cranshaws village before recrossing it. There is a small castle at Cranshaws but not really accessible by car, actually not a castle but one of the usual border pele towers incorporated in a farm, about half a mile west of Cranshaws church and reached by a lane.

Soon we reach Ellemford, where we again cross the river, by a three-arched stone bridge, and go straight on beyond the bridge through an afforested valley. We temporarily leave the course of the Whiteadder but, after about three miles, rejoin it and cross it after forking left at a bridge for Chirnside. The noble White-adder valley of the hills has become a comparatively flat river valley as we join a main road into Preston, going through the village, and at its other end bear right (being very careful at the blind corner) for Chirnside. Thereafter we continue towards Chirnside until after a sharp corner we go straight on for Edrom where the Chirnside road turns left, downhill to cross the White-adder once more and on its other side turn through a hairpin bend uphill, crossing a subsequent main road and bearing left at the next junction through a wood and over the relatively level

landscape where the Lammermuir is only a dim outline. Our last
glimpse of the Whiteadder is when we cross a tributary but turn
away from the bridge over the Whiteadder into Allanton, through
the long village street and on to a major crossroads, which we
cross for Coldstream.

At the next T-junction we turn left for Norham and soon cross
A699 into an unsignposted minor road. Now the dominant
feature in the landscape is the Cheviot ahead. After about one
and a half miles we turn right for Swinton but only follow this
road for a quarter of a mile then turn left in an unsignposted lane,
which requires careful navigation to spot it, continuing to the
next T-junction, where our way is to the right by the wall of
Ladykirk House. We follow the park wall to the left for Coldstream at a T-junction, passing one of the imposing entrances to
the park. Ignoring a turning on the right which is signposted
Coldstream, we make the best of both worlds by going straight
on along the way which is also signposted Coldstream and
brings us quickly to the banks of the Tweed, a lovely road with
incomparable river views and one grand surprise view when we
first approach it.

So we enter Coldstream and turn left on the Berwick road, but
it is certainly well worth while to drive into the town down the
main street and back again to see one of the many towns in
Scotland which are predominantly Georgian and contrive to
retain their Georgian flavour. It is a mere incident in its long
history that General Monk raised the first Coldstream Guards
here in 1660 and there is little to commemorate this famous fact.
The monument, which one might have expected to have been of
the great general, is to Charles Marjoribanks, one-time M.P. for
the County of Berwick, allied with the parliamentary victory of
1832, the year of the great Reform Bill. His statue on a high
column towers over the town and the Tweed, which we cross by
a stone bridge into England and drive on to Cornhill.

At a roundabout beyond Cornhill we bear right for Wooler,
continuing for about one and a half miles, then turn right again
on the way signposted Branxton, where we drive past the little
church and take a hairpin bend to the right to the site of Flodden
Field, where in 1513 James IV was killed at a time when it seemed
as though the war between England and Scotland would continue
for ever. A rather meagre monument reached by steps and a

footpath from the road marks this great event. Beyond it we reach a T-junction where we turn right, and right again at the next T-junction and hard left at a war memorial about 100 yards further for Kelso. The rest is simple. The Kelso road is an extraordinarily pleasant one, sometimes wooded, sometimes completely open and looking across the Tweed to the southern uplands. There are occasional glimpses of the river, especially near Wark, where there was once a great castle by the river, now only a scanty fragment. We re-enter Scotland after Carham, where the boundary veers south away from the line of the Tweed, and so through Sprouston, the only other sizeable village before Kelso.

The next tour, which links the Tweed valley with the Moorfoot Hills, is just under 100 miles in length and includes some of the finest scenery which may loosely be called border scenery and in addition contains many intimate glimpses of famous places, especially in the first few miles, when we pass Mellerstain, one of the finest of Scottish houses which are open to the public. Although the tour is routed from Kelso, it is equally easy to follow from the Scott country, especially such centres as Selkirk or Melrose. With only a few miles added it comes within the compass of a day's ride from Hawick or Jedburgh, or even Edinburgh, from which at our nearest point we are little more than 12 miles away.

If the start is at Kelso we leave by Roxburgh Street and pass the park of Floors Castle, as on the previous route (A6089). At the end of the park wall we turn left for Earlston on B6397. Neglecting two left turns, we leave this road for a turning on the left, B6404, signposted St Boswells. Smailholm Tower is our immediate objective, one of the best preserved and certainly one of the most spectacular of medieval fortified homes, which we soon see set high on a rock outcrop ahead of us. Its very position demands that we should approach it, if not explore it. In about one and a half miles we turn right along a very obscure unsignposted lane, the tower now on our left, then bear left at the first unsignposted T-junction, which takes us to Sandyknowe farmhouse. A rough track goes on beyond the farmhouse to the tower, though the view of it from here cannot be bettered. The keys can be obtained from the farmhouse and for anyone interested in a fifteenth-century fortified yeoman's house it is an absolute must. Scott was a frequent visitor as a boy, when the farm was occupied by his grandparents, and the tower is featured in his *Marmion*.

Resuming our way, we return to the public road and go straight ahead between low stone walls with a fine view of the Eildon Hills away to our left. At a T-junction outside Smailholm village we turn right into it then left in its centre for Earlston on B6397, and at the next T-junction bear right for Mellerstain, which is open on all summer afternoons except Saturdays and is approached by a magnificent avenue. Mellerstain, the home of the Earls of Haddington, is often described as the finest Adam house in Scotland. It is indeed a composite of two of the most famous Adams, the centre block having been built by Robert between 1760 and 1770 and the two wings by his father William about 1725, while most of the interior decoration is by Robert. Its most famous feature is the plaster work in the ceilings of many of its rooms, while its Italianate gardens are among the most ornate in Scotland. Altogether it is a house to see if at all possible. We actually pass two entrances and go forward for Gordon on A6089, turning left to Gordon and there left again for Earlston, in just over half a mile passing a magnificent tower house known as Greenknowe Tower, which dates from the sixteenth century and, though roofless, is otherwise virtually intact.

After 2 more miles, just beyond a hamlet, we fork right in an unsignposted narrow and rather rough road, which approaches the 800-ft contour then enters a dense wood, a road which is beautified by the flowering hedgerows of rosebay willowherb in season. When we reach the next T-junction we turn right and gradually ascend towards the summit of the Moorfoot Hills, going straight on at the next crossroads for Boon by a group of farm buildings, but soon take a right fork for Dods and turn right at a T-junction where Boon Hill (1,070 ft) is immediately on our left. So we descend to a major road in a valley, where we bear left towards Lauder and cross Boondreigh Water, following this road as far as its junction with the Edinburgh road, where we fork right. It makes little difference actually whether we take this way or go forward through Lauder then turn right in the trunk road but though Lauderdale is romantic and interesting, Lauder itself has relatively little of interest except a distinguished town hall and a late-sixteenth-

century church and it is scarcely worth undertaking the extra
miles of trunk road in order to see it.

If we take the first turning signposted Edinburgh our road
runs well above the valley of the Leader Water looking down on
the woodlands of Thirlestane Castle, which is hidden among them,
and continues to Carfraemill, where we bear right again for
Edinburgh, now on the trunk road A68, climbing steeply over
bare hills and reaching a height of nearly 1,200 ft. However,
when we have crossed the summit, from which there is a long
view over the coastal plain, we soon leave the main road on
B6368, which is signposted Galashiels. For a time the landscape
is bleak, almost treeless, but later we come to heather-covered
slopes which in the late summer and autumn make the Moorfoot
Hills almost as colourful as the Lammermuir. The Armet winds
down the valley beside us to join the Gala Water, the banks of
which we reach at another major road, A7, across which we look
to the main massif of the Moorfoots.

We turn right in the latter road, which in spite of the weight of
traffic it carries occasionally is a charming and picturesque road,
and continue on it for between four and five miles. This takes
us over another watershed, beyond which our view is forward
into the fertile acres of Midlothian. Just short of a wood we
turn left for Innerleithen on B7007, driving over the very summit
of the Moorfoots and several times rising above the 1,300-ft
contour, one of the most exciting rides in the hills of the southern
uplands and the border country. Once again the landscape is
bleak in the extreme, for a time with only bog and rank grass on
the hillsides, but presently heather once more makes its appearance and transverse ravines break up the monotony of the
featureless hills on our left. Later we bear left on B709 for Heriot
parallel with Heriot Water, which here has been joined by several
other streams. As we reach the lower ground the heather is
more luxuriant, the landscapes kinder. Continuing, we rejoin
the valley of Gala Water, a still more fertile valley with good
pasture on the lower slopes and scarcely a hint of the sternness of
the scenery towards the summit of the Moorfoots.

We cross Heriot Water twice, passing Heriot's picturesque
little church, then turn sharp right before actually reaching Gala
Water, a difficult manoeuvre, not in the sense of requiring any
particular driving skill but a turning which it is extraordinarily

easy to miss. Our aim is to drive down the valley of Gala Water
with the river on our left. If we miss this turning we cross it and
come to the main road. In that case the only thing to do is to turn
back and try again. At the point at which we turn right we can
actually see the main road and the railway across the valley.
You will know you have gone too far if you reach Heriot station
about a quarter of a mile beyond our turning.

It is an easy ride down the Gala Water, and a very lovely one
towards Galashiels, with the river in a deep glen on the left.
When the valley begins to flatten out another road joins ours and
we enter Fountainhall village. Soon, however, we are once more
high above the glen, riding beside hanging woods which reach
down to the very bank of the river. Beyond the woods we can
see Stow, a large village with a spired church, on the further side
of the river, then cross Lugate Water by a fine stone bridge,
keeping left so as to maintain our course as closely as possible to
the Gala and turning left at the first obvious road junction. So
we actually cross Gala Water, passing under a railway bridge,
and emerge finally on the main road, A7, in which we turn right,
following it for about three miles towards Galashiels, now on the
east bank of the river. Then we turn left for Langshaw over a
shoulder of William Law, continuing to a T-junction at the
further side of a little wood where the way to Langshaw bears
right. When we reach this tiny hamlet we turn left for Earlston,
soon passing yet another fine tower house or pele tower with
surrounding wall (remarkably like the Irish castle and bawn)
and soon find our way to Earlston through well-wooded
country.

We descend into Lauderdale, in which we turn right at a
T-junction in the midst of woods, then bear left across Leader
Water into Earlston, thereafter crossing a main road, driving
through the pleasant square of the town and continuing to the
next signposted fork in about one and a quarter miles, whence
the way to Kelso is well signposted on B6397. There is never a
dull moment in these last few miles and you will be unlucky if
you meet more than two or three cars using the road before you
reach Kelso.

The last tour in this chapter takes us to many of the places
associated with the life and death of Sir Walter Scott and some
which he specially loved, as well as to the outliers of Ettrick

Forest and many miles of the broad waters of the Tweed and Teviot. It is strictly speaking an historic tour but has so much beauty in it that motorists who have no interest at all in border legends, or for that matter in history, will find it interesting and rewarding. Earlston is its logical starting point but Earlston unfortunately is not a place at which there is accommodation for visitors in quantity. Selkirk and Jedburgh are the nearest places with hotel and boarding-house facilities, and there is always Kelso, one of the best centres of all for the Scott country and the Tweed valley. Melrose is another possible centre. It is not so long a tour as most of those in this book—a mere 80 miles if the start is made at Kelso, rather less from Selkirk or Jedburgh. That is to allow time for seeing the ruins of three abbeys, Jedburgh, Melrose and Dryburgh (apart from Kelso, seen on another tour), and the many other features of interest which inevitably take time yet should not be missed if a balanced view is to be obtained of this romantic countryside. The way from Kelso to Earlston is by Smailholm on A6089 and B6397. Readers from Jedburgh and Selkirk, or Melrose, will do best to join the route in its middle and follow it as described.

In Earlston's spacious square we take the turn which is sign-posted Bemersyde and Scott's View. In fact the local signposting appears to be very keen that we should not miss Scott's View, which is signposted a number of times in the next few miles. The road, numbered B6356, climbs through hanging woods under the slopes of prominent hills which the ordnance survey reveals as White Hill and Black Hill. Later the way is signposted Dryburgh.

One could be forgiven if one thought that too much was made of this famous viewpoint but it would be difficult to overrate the beauty of a place which was one of Sir Walter's favourite view-points. Immediately below it runs the Tweed, beyond it the three summits of the Eildon Hills, which rise to between 1,200 and 1,350 ft, though from here they look much higher. An indicator by the car park shows many famous places. One can well believe that Scott was right when he said that it was possible from the summit of the highest of the Eildons to see 43 places 'famous in war and verse'.

We continue beyond the viewpoint on a road which is always interesting round a shoulder of Bemersyde Hill, ultimately reaching Dryburgh Abbey, which is on a byway still well sign-posted. Sir Walter Scott is buried in Dryburgh, a Premonstra-tensian abbey founded in the twelfth century, almost totally destroyed during the Earl of Hertford's campaign in 1544, and never rebuilt. So, although the ruins of the church and the conventual buildings are both interesting and picturesque, it was a ruin in which Sir Walter Scott was laid to rest in 1832 and in which his wife and son are also buried.

Returning from the abbey, we bear right past the post office and keep right at the next T-junction for St Boswells and soon see the Tweed, thereafter continuing to St Boswells, turning right in the next hamlet and right at a subsequent T-junction. The bridge over the Tweed is a high one, giving fine views on each side of it of the river bounded by wooded red cliffs with the Eildons well to the right. After that we traverse the small town or large village of St Boswells and reaching a major road beyond its pleasant green bear right for Melrose on A6091. And so to Melrose by way of Newtown, briefly joining A68 but soon leaving it for A6091, which takes us under the steep slopes of the Eildons.

Melrose is a very gracious place, a handsome town with an ancient market cross in its central square and many fine seventeenth- and eighteenth-century houses. Its real pride is the abbey, which is signposted on our right as we enter the market square, a beautiful red sandstone building which must move even the least appreciative to real admiration, though it is in ruins. This was a Cistercian abbey and unhappily the church is the only substantial part of it which remains, though the foundations of many of the conventual buildings have been uncovered. It was founded by King David I, its first monks being called from Rievaulx in Yorkshire. It was always regarded as the successor of a far more ancient monastery which had flourished in Melrose in the early Middle Ages. Like so many others of southern Scotland's monasteries, it was burnt to the ground during the wars with England and virtually ceased to exist in 1385, but it was rebuilt in the fifteenth century, from which the greater part of the lovely church dates. There is a tradition that the heart of Robert Bruce is buried in the church but no one has been bold enough to identify the site.

We return from the abbey to the market place and continue our previous direction for a time towards Galashiels. Abbotsford,

our next objective, is almost as well signposted as was Scott's
View and we shall have no difficulty in finding it. The way takes
us along the Tweed valley, here at its finest. Later we fork left
for Abbotsford and Selkirk, soon reaching the home of Sir
Walter Scott, or rather the home which he built for himself and
in which he died in 1832, and has become famous above all other
homes of his. Its principal interest is that it is genuinely the work
of Sir Walter, the artist, for he designed and supervised every
phase of its building between 1821 and his death, and incidentally
is said to have planted every tree in the estate in which it stands.
So one must regard it as expressing the great novelist's person-
ality, though its many turrets and its elaborate interior decoration
certainly do not accord with modern taste in every detail. Even
so, it is impressive and the collection of Scott relics is a most
interesting one.

Beyond the house we follow the course of the Tweed into
Selkirk, turning left at the T-junction with A7 for the last two
miles. The spired town hall and court house is Selkirk's most
conspicuous building, with Scott's statue outside. Here Sir
Walter administered justice as Sheriff from 1803 to 1832. Further
down the High Street is the statue of Mungo Park, the explorer.
We turn right by the town hall and market cross downhill
towards Ettrick Water, then left for Ettrick short of the river,
climbing temporarily away from it then back beside it to a left
turn (prohibited to heavy traffic and about two miles from
Selkirk) rising steeply away from the river valley. We continue
on this minor road, bearing left at the first junction, over fine
moorland with grand views to our left, a foretaste of the beauties
of Ettrick Forest. At a major road by Ale Water, to which we
bear left, we turn right along it for a long mile, taking the
second turning on the left, a pleasant little road which after
climbing over a hill reaches a T-junction by a farmhouse where we
turn right, and right again at a subsequent T-junction, following
this road to the outskirts of Lilliesleaf, then right for Hawick on
B6359, and right after two miles at a T-junction, again signposted
Hawick. The prominent outline of the Minto Hills (two peaks
that appear almost as one) is on our left, with lovely rounded
summits. At another T-junction we turn left for Denholm,
steering towards these magnificent hills and shortly afterwards
forking left, subsequently turning right at a T-junction by farms

through the little village of Minto, with its unexpectedly large
towered church, and left at the next junction along a fine avenue
of trees. Now we are approaching the valley of the Teviot, which
is our guide for the rest of the tour. At the first T-junction we
turn left along it. There are many handsome views of the river,
which here is almost as mighty a river as the Tweed, which it
joins just below Kelso. For much of its lower course its banks
are wooded, the woods occasionally interrupted by abrupt cliffs.
Everywhere it is totally unspoilt and always lovely.

In a few miles we reach Ancrum, where we temporarily leave
the Teviot for a detour to the historic border town of Jedburgh,
bearing right for Nisbet on B6400 and shortly bearing right
again at the major road on the other side of a bridge over a
tributary stream. After that we follow A68 into Jedburgh which,
were it not a place firmly astride A68, would be an infinitely
more attractive town than it is. Even so, it is well worth a visit,
principally to see the red sandstone remains of its abbey, which
was founded early in the twelfth century by King David I and,
like many other famous buildings we pass, was badly damaged
during the campaign of the Earl of Hertford in 1544-1545. Its
real beauty is its Norman work and the Norman nave of the
abbey church, consisting of nine bays which illustrate admirably
the transition between Norman and Gothic. Unfortunately little
remains of the claustral buildings.

The same is true of Jedburgh Castle, which was one of the most
powerful in the lowlands in the twelfth, thirteenth and fourteenth
centuries but was destroyed in 1409 because the Scottish raiders
regarded it as of more value to the English than to the Scots, the
best possible reason they could have had for destroying it. One
other link with the past, however, exists in Queen Mary's house,
in which the unhappy Queen was staying when she visited
Bothwell in Hermitage Castle in 1566 (see page 47), the occasion
on which the arduous ride almost proved fatal to her. It is one of
the most interesting houses open to the public in Scotland and is
now used as a museum, though the museum is less interesting
than the house itself.

We leave Jedburgh by A68 for Kelso, bearing right at the first
fork for Kelso on A6090 which almost immediately joins A698.
After one and a half miles, however, we leave this broad highway
for a turn on the left which is signposted Nisbet and brings us

The cliffs and stack rock of Whitley Bay.   (Chapter 5.)

The harbour of the ancient fishing village of Seahouses.   (Chapter 5.)

The three peaks of the Eildon Hills from Scott's View, the novelist's favourite viewpoint. (Chapter 6.)

The ruins of the Cistercian abbey of Melrose. (Chapter 6.)

back to the banks of the Teviot. The high column of the Waterloo
Monument, which we have seen in the distance many times
during the day, stands on its abrupt hill above Nisbet. It was
built in 1815 by the Marquis of Lothian and his tenants. Soon we
turn right for Roxburgh at a T-junction, driving through charming woodlands with one or two outstanding views across the
valley of the Teviot to the distant Tweedsmuir Hills, and after
passing under a railway bridge go forward into Roxburgh.

It is difficult to tell the story of Roxburgh in a few words.
Now it is obviously a small village with the unsubstantial ruins
of a castle by the river. It is very hard to re-create the time when
it was one of four royal burghs in Scotland, of which the other
three were Edinburgh, Stirling and Berwick, which we cannot
really count as a Scottish town. But that was in the thirteenth
century when the castle was a royal residence to which Alexander
II was a frequent visitor and in which Alexander III was born
in 1231.

From this point the signposts show the way to Kelso, which is
to the right on A699, a very pleasant way with a good view of the
junction of the Tweed and Teviot and the unexpected view of
Floors Castle and its park across the water. We cross the Teviot
for the last time before its junction with the Tweed.

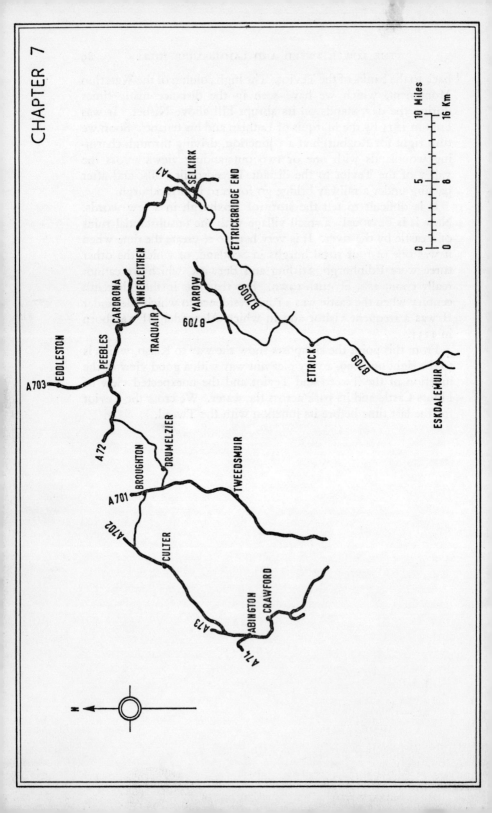

CHAPTER SEVEN

THE UPPER TWEED AND ETTRICK FOREST

IN THIS CHAPTER we visit some of the most beautiful places in the southern uplands of Scotland. The country between the valley of the upper Tweed from its source downstream as far as the Scott country, and the equally distinguished valley of the Ettrick Water, are at first glance rather far from the English-Scottish border to deserve the name border country. Yet this is the very area which has attracted to itself most border songs and ballads, especially the now sadly neglected poems of James Hogg, who brought to life the very spirit of the land and who is remembered now by a number of monuments which we shall visit.

The source of the Tweed is in the hills only a few miles from Moffat and the Devil's Beef Tub, one of the most dramatic of all the combes in the uplands, which by a strange conservatism most Scots call lowlands to distinguish them from the highlands to the north of Edinburgh, even though many of the peaks in the Tweedsmuir range rise to nearly 3,000 ft and the scenery, especially in August and September when the heather is ablaze, is unlike anything else in the whole of Great Britain. Though the Tweed is without doubt a border river, the Clyde, which rises less than a mile away from it, is one of the great rivers of Scotland and has no historic link with the border country.

No one can say where the influence of the border, or rather of the turmoil and strife of centuries which mark the wars between England and Scotland for possession of the border, begins or ends. A great many of the places we shall visit on the tours in this chapter are very very Scottish. Indeed in a sense they all are, just as Northumberland, in spite of its proximity to the nominal border line, is very very English. It is as though nationality were accentuated by the discord and by the wars which rendered its exact position always so doubtful.

Our first tour is a relatively short one, completing in effect the survey of the Moorfoot Hills which was started in a previous chapter and also seeing one of the loveliest stretches of the upper Tweed. The best centre for starting and ending it is Peebles, though Innerleithen is almost as good, and it is within easy reach of the several towns and villages with accommodation in the Scott country lower down the Tweed, in Selkirk or Melrose or Dryburgh, or even in Galashiels.

Peebles, in any case, is a most interesting town quite apart from being an admirable touring centre and has what so many of the towns of southern Scotland have not, an abundance of accommodation. It has peculiarly Scottish associations, for it was a place beloved by the early kings of Scotland, especially Alexander III, who had a hunting lodge in the immediate vicinity. Its Feast of Beltane, a celebration of very early origin, is still maintained but nothing remains of the old town, which was destroyed by English armies at least twice and was finally quelled by Cromwell's army in 1649. However, there are a number of seventeenth-century buildings, including the 'Cross Keys' inn, which was previously a private house, and the Chambers Institute, which formerly belonged to the Queensberry family. Only the Tweed bridge can genuinely claim to be older, and this was built certainly in the fifteenth century, if not before; that, and the remains of the Cross Kirk (principally the tower) which dates from 1261. The shaft of the town cross is also early, though its exact date is unknown. But it is impossible to describe Peebles in terms of its buildings; its appeal is mainly that of atmosphere, the very epitome of a Scottish lowland town, proud and steeped in history but always modest.

We leave it by the Traquair road, crossing the Tweed bridge and following the road beside the river, soon leaving all sign of the town and coming out into a reach where the Tweedsmuirs rise steeply on our right and the wooded foothills of the Moor- foots dominate the landscape across the river, to which the road at times comes down and at others rides on a shelf high above it. After a short distance through woods we emerge into the open at Cardrona, just beyond which we look across the Tweed to Innerleithen and the valley of the Leithen Water snaking into the Moorfoot Hills.

That is our next objective, but first we pass the always closed Bear Gates of Traquair House which, tradition has it, were shut in 1796 on the death of the last Countess. Traquair is generally described as the oldest inhabited house in Scotland and one which has certainly remained largely unaltered for more than 300 years. It is well worth seeing and is open to the public during the summer months in the afternoon. Its traditions are so positively Jacobite that it would be surprising if one's guide to Traquair did not also have Jacobite sympathies. Incidentally, the brew house dates from the eighteenth century and is said to be the only one in Scotland of a comparable kind which is licensed to brew and sell its unique product, Traquair ale.

On reaching a major road at Traquair village we turn left for Innerleithen, which we reach after crossing the Tweed, bearing right in the town as for Galashiels but near its end turn left for Heriot up the Leithen valley, quickly coming to the heart of the Moorfoot Hills. The Leithen is a lovely river bubbling over its stony bed as it flows close beside the road. There are many lovely and varied views up the valley itself and along transverse ones. When we say goodbye to the Leithen we follow the valley of a tributary stream, with the bold summit of Whitehope Law (2,038 ft) on our left. Soon we begin to ascend more steeply, with the stream cascading noisily beside us and an ever more desolate landscape in which the sheep and their circular pens are the main signs of human intervention.

When we have crossed the summit the descent is much more gradual, our road crossing the Dewar burn several times before it joins the valley of Heriot Water. At a junction we go forward for Gorebridge, climbing high over a naked summit with a glimpse up the narrow Blackhope valley to its several isolated farms. At the highest point of the pass we reach 1,324 ft. Then as we begin the final descent of the Moorfoots we are rewarded with a superb view towards the Firth of Forth, a silver streak ahead. In clear weather the dim outline of the highlands can be made out beyond it. Equally it is possible to identify Arthur's Seat and the Salisbury Crags, and the rock on which Edinburgh's castle is set.

As our road begins to flatten out at the foot of the hill we fork left at the first junction, continuing beside park lands on our right to a crossroads, where our way is again to the left down a pretty little valley, bearing left once more, for Outerston, soon after passing a lime works, apparently of ancient foundation, with disused kilns (neglecting a farm road over a cattle grid). At the next junction also we turn left, soon coming to the shore of

the Gladhouse reservoir. The shore of the reservoir is fringed
with conifers and, like so many other reservoir scenes, looks like the
work of nature. We turn right along it, crossing a bridge beside
the steep outflow. Then at a crossroads by a letterbox after
leaving the shores of the lake we turn left, now skirting the foot
of the hills and continuing for several miles to a major road, in
which we bear left for a long two miles as far as Eddleston,
where we are in the valley of Eddleston Water. Here we turn
right where the signpost reads Lyne and the 'Black Barony' hotel,
turning left at the hotel entrance, soon climbing high above the
valley for a grand view of the Tweedsmuir Hills ahead across
the waterway of the Tweed. It is a wild moorland landscape and
its desolation is relieved by large areas of heather and by the
great number of sheep which miraculously find good grazing
amid this desolation.

At the first junction we take the left fork (though both forks
emerge on the major road to Peebles) and left again, reaching
this major road, a very lovely one which closely follows the bank
of the Tweed. A grand detour, if time permits, begins just
beyond a large quarry on our left and is signposted Manor Kirk.
This road ascends the valley of Manor Water into the very heart
of the Tweedsmuir Hills to within walking distance of St Mary's
Loch over the high pass. It is a walk which commands exceptional
views and is well worth while for the energetic and fit. The path
is well marked but let no one think that it is a half hour's walk.
From the point where the road ends to Cappercleugh, the nearest
point on St Mary's Loch, is nearly seven miles and the track,
which starts at an altitude of well under 1,000 ft, ascends to not
far short of 2,000 ft before descending to loch level, which is
about 800 ft. It is really a day's work in itself, though a very
lovely one. Whether we are strong walkers or not, the ride up
Manor Water is easy and rewarding.

We must return to the main road, passing Neidpath Castle
before entering Peebles. The castle, which is open during the
summer months, is exceptionally well preserved and takes some
of its attraction from its magnificent position virtually over-
hanging the Tweed. The ancient tower is incorporated in a
rather more modern castle-like residence but the effect is of a
medieval stronghold, which incidentally was acquired by the
1st Duke of Queensberry in the latter part of the seventeenth

century. The 4th Duke ('Old Q') was apostrophized by Words-
worth in a sonnet as a degenerate Douglas because he elected to
clear the view by felling the timber immediately surrounding
the castle. As we enter Peebles we pass the tower of Cross Kirk,
and so end a tour amounting to about seventy miles if the detour
up the Manor Water is followed, a mere 50 miles if the direct
route is taken.

The next tour, of just under 100 miles, includes the most
varied of the Tweedsmuir Hills, takes us to the source of the
Tweed, which unlike that of the Clyde is a known entity, and
past the Devil's Beef Tub and that other deservedly well-known
beauty spot, St Mary's Loch. It also includes one or two byways
which very few motorists drive over but which reveal the
scenery in all its majesty, for the appeal of the tour is chiefly
scenic and there are only a few places along the 100 miles which
can reasonably be called places of historic note.

It is routed from Peebles, but Innerleithen is just as good a
starting point and, as we said at the beginning of the previous
tour, Innerleithen itself is so near the principal centres of the
Scott country, Selkirk, Melrose and Dryburgh, that it can easily
be undertaken from any of those, while after the Devil's Beef Tub
it comes within five miles of Moffat, which makes yet another
possible centre, as do the primarily fishing inns, such as the
'Gordon Arms' and 'Tibbie Shiel's', described later.

Starting at Peebles we shall take the opportunity of exploring the left bank, that is, by A72, which hugs this bank closely
and in many ways is a finer road than the byway on the other
bank though naturally there are times when it carries more
traffic than permits a really leisurely exploration. Its great virtue
is that from the left bank the views are always across the river to
the Tweedsmuirs, which take on all the stature of mountains
when viewed from river level. By this way, too, we pass the
tower of Horsburgh Castle on our right about midway between
Peebles and Innerleithen. In the latter we turn right for Traquair,
crossing the Tweed and neglecting the road on the left which is
signposted Elibank. But because we neglect it today is no reason
for doing so on some other occasion, for it is the key to four
miles of most attractive motoring along the right bank of the
river, remarkably quiet, one might almost say unknown, bringing
us back to A72 only about six miles from Selkirk, so that it

provides an alternative way for an approach to the tour from the
latter. Motorists who do, in fact, start at Selkirk and follow A72
in order to join the tour must turn left where the signpost reads
Peel Hospital, a perfectly accurate but rather misleading signpost.
Certainly it is a ride which on no account should be missed.

To resume our route, we continue for St Mary's Loch and
Traquair, passing one of the main entrances to Traquair House,
and at Traquair post office go forward for Ettrick, following the
shallow valley of the Quair Water and later that of the Newhall
burn, which takes us through heather slopes to the watershed and
into what is a pass in the true sense of the term, for our road
rises to 1,170 ft under Mountbenger (1,784 ft), a rounded hill
which towers on our left. As we descend the Mountbenger
burn runs on our left through a number of small ravines. At the
foot of the pass we find ourselves in the famous valley of the
Yarrow, and justly famous it is.

At the 'Gordon Arms' hotel we turn right for St Mary's Loch,
keeping close to the Yarrow valley with the Yarrow Water
beside us nearly all the way to the loch, the shore of which we
skirt closely as far as the point where the road bends south.
Every vista is enhanced by the loch and though the height
above sea-level of its water is not less than 800 ft the surrounding
green hills look for all the world like mountains in their own right.

The main road continues along the shore (we shall be returning
to it on another tour) but we turn right where the signpost reads
Tweedsmuir to follow the Megget Water along a road which
until a few years ago was a narrow untarred one but is now
beautifully surfaced with passing places, often quite unnecessary,
at intervals. There is, however, one point after a few miles where
the surface of the road is still admirable but widening it has so far
proved too much of an obstacle to the local authorities to perform.
We rise gradually, passing several farms, but soon the moors
open out without a sign of habitation. On our way we pass the
end of the 'public footpath' which leads to the Manor Water and
is signposted (this was referred to in the previous tour) then pass
under the steep slopes of Dollar Law (2,680 ft) and Broad Law
(2,754 ft), the highest summit in the Tweedsmuirs and only
overtopped in southern Scotland by Merrick, high set among the
Galloway mountains. Our road achieves a height of almost
1,500 ft as we pass under the lower slopes of Broad Law, which

here is barren and scree-covered, before descending steeply to the Talla Water and at once have a really magnificent view of the Talla reservoir, a long narrow sheet of water between precipitous green slopes broken by screes.

Crossing the head of the reservoir, we follow the road along its shore, crossing a dam at the approach to Victoria Lodge, where the grounds are surprisingly rich in lovely rhododendrons and woods, soon descending to the Tweed valley and the village of Tweedsmuir, which we shall recognize on our right by the little spired church on an artificial mound which may well bespeak an origin far earlier than that of the present fabric.

Crossing the infant Tweed, we turn left in a major road towards Moffat and watch the Tweed, already a narrow river, transform itself into a tiny stream and eventually die out among apparently impenetrable bogs just before we pass the signpost which points the way improbably to the source of the Tweed. Soon afterwards we come to the natural bowl of the Devil's Beef Tub and after crossing the next bridge over a deep ravine turn right, signposted Abington, continuing over bare moorland but descending gradually to the level of the main road A74, the only road in this part of Scotland which carries traffic comparable with that of many English main roads and with its dual carriageway is almost as swift and almost as ugly. However, ugly or not, we must follow it briefly because it is in effect the only road through the pass and paralleled by the railway beside it which carries the main line from Glasgow to Carlisle.

It is a matter of about ten miles at the most before we leave it, turning right to drive through Crawford, which we find to be a pleasant but not particularly distinguished village, and at its end turn right where the signpost reads Crawford Castle, crossing the railway and river (one of the headwaters of the Clyde) and turning right at a T-junction to find the fragment of the castle, Tower Lindsay, as it is more usually called, now a mere fragment on a mound in the midst of trees a quarter of a mile from the T-junction. Returning to the T-junction we go straight ahead (i.e. turning left if we do not go to Tower Lindsay), skirting the bold green Castle Hill then driving through woodlands, turning left after 2 miles at the end of a belt of woodlands towards a farm (the promising-looking road ahead leads only to the fields) soon crossing the railway and the river.

So we reach a major road at Abington and turn right in it
(A73) but a long mile further, where this major road forks left,
bear right towards Biggar on A702, continuing on this fairly wide
but seldom busy road as far as Culter, where we turn right then
left for Broughton along an extremely beautiful byway which
looks across a wide valley to Biggar and the hills beyond.
Ultimately we reach another main road, A701, where we turn
right for a short mile and left into the turning which is signposted
Peebles.

There is no real difficulty about this part of the tour once we
have achieved the right road from Abington. All we have to bear
in mind is that Biggar is too far to the left and Broughton the
point at which we join the wider road. In many parts the landscape has a park-like quality which certainly adds enormously to
the beauty of the ride. Now that we are guided by Peebles signposts the difficulty is even less. We pass through Drumelzier,
which has a ruined castle near the Tweed though its ruins are far
too fragmentary to be seen from the road, then see the more
conspicuous ruins of Tinnis Castle on a high hill promontory
above the road on our right.

Soon we reach the Tweed valley, crossing the river then going
on for Peebles through magnificent woodlands, coming into the
open briefly before we reach A72 4 miles from Peebles centre.
It is a really lovely ride which shows one of the best stretches of
the Tweed valley and proves this to be as splendid a river valley
as any in the southern half of Scotland.

The next tour is to the country of the Ettrick shepherd,
James Hogg, who was steeped in border legends and wrote a
great number of memorable poems which the present generation
is forgetting though most Scottish people over forty regard him
with something of the veneration usually reserved for Burns.
What Hogg did was to bring the reality of border feuds and
rivalries into the nineteenth century and make them part and parcel
of the countryside. So in a special sense Hogg's country is the
border country *par excellence*, and very lovely country it is, with
not a single jarring note in the tour which follows, extending to
just over a hundred miles.

The best place at which to begin it is Selkirk, although it is
perfectly feasible to plan the start from Peebles or Innerleithen,
from Melrose, or from any of the small towns in the Scott country.

If we come from Peebles or Innerleithen the best way is to cross the hills by B709 as far as the 'Gordon Arms' and there turn left into Selkirk, after that following the tour as described. Otherwise we make first for Selkirk and there leave its high-set market place on the Peebles road, dropping steeply downhill by West Port towards Ettrick Water but short of the river turning left for Ettrick on B7009 along Ettrick Road. It is a wonderfully easy escape from the town, every sign of which has disappeared before we have gone 2 miles. Not only that, but there are grand views along the valley at once. Our road keeps close to the river, which we avoid crossing by a single-arched bridge on the right. About a mile beyond the bridge Oakwood Tower, a conspicuous landmark on a hill to our left, is an early seventeenth-century construction. The Ettrick Water flows through a deep wooded glen before we leave it for a time to drive through the bare uplands. It is almost with relief that we rejoin the course of the river at Ettrick bridge and there cross it in the midst of luxuriant woodlands, going through the attractive village of Ettrickbridge and continuing along the river's other bank, from which very soon we have a fine view of the wooded cliff on its further side. From now on we are never far from the stream; the temptations to cross it are numerous but all the little roads which do so end at farmhouses among the hills.

As we go upstream the landscape becomes more dramatic, with heather-covered moors taking the place of the wooded slopes lower downstream. Presently we reach a belt of woodland and join B709 for Langholm, but this road, like so many B roads in the south of Scotland, carries practically no traffic and is in every sense a byway. We pass the 'Tushielaw' inn, continuing for Langholm, with Ettrick Pen (2,270 ft) the most conspicuous summit ahead of us, later forking right into Ettrick. Here the kirk where James Hogg is buried lies just off the road. An obelisk with a plaque in relief of an excellent head and shoulders portrait of him, and decorated with rams' heads and garlands, is on the site of the cottage where he was born in 1770 (he died in 1835). Incidentally, the churchyard is said to contain also the gravestone of Tibbie Shiel (Isabella Richardson), 1783-1878, the famous innkeeper of the 'Tibbie Shiel's' inn where De Quincey and other famous literary figures foregathered. The discouraging notice 'No through road' deters many from driving to near the headwaters of the Ettrick. It is a lovely drive which no one should miss, nearly seven miles from the church to the furthest point to which the road can be followed. It is a narrow road generously supplied with passing places; the scenery through which it passes is superb. It ends at a good turning place by a small quarry and goes no further than the farm which can be seen ahead, though strong walkers, of course, can walk over the hill to within sight of Moffat within an hour. In every way, the scenery is typical of the finest that the southern uplands of Scotland can offer.

In any case, we must return to Ettrick village and the main road B709, in which we turn right, crossing the Ettrick Water to follow one of its tributaries, the Tima Water. The valley becomes narrower as we ascend, riding between the low green hills, rather bare and almost devoid of heather, though recent afforestation higher up the valley relieves the scenery of any tedium. At its highest point our road exceeds 1,250 ft, then gradually descends into the valley of the White Esk and becomes relatively broad and fertile. In quiet weather the river is a mere trickle though the stones along its course and its wide sandy bed suggest what it is like when in spate.

Soon we pass the entrance to the Eskdalemuir observatory, which on many occasions has recorded the lowest official temperatures in Great Britain, and later come to the tiny village and small spired church, by which we turn right for Lockerbie on B723, climbing again into a splendid mountain vista and going through the dense forest of Twiglees. We follow the valley of the Black Esk for a while, the river far below us and at Boreland village continue on B723, still for Lockerbie. Soon, however, we fork right for Wamphray along a very pretty byway which takes us once more over the moors with the Galloway Hills far seen on the western landscape. As we descend Annandale comes into view before us, with the Lowther and Tinto Hills bounding it on its further side. The scenery is as different as could be imagined from that of the moors we have left behind us. Everything is peaceful and often sunny when the hills are cloud-covered. It is rich farming country with fields under oats and barley and many fine herds of cattle grazing in the meadows by the riverside.

We turn right at a T-junction beside the river over a bridge and straight on by Pumplaburn Farm, keeping as near as possible to the valley, with the hills on our right. We only leave Annandale when we reach the Moffat Water and the Annan river is hidden behind a low green ridge. We turn right beside a mature wood just short of a bridge over the Moffat Water (if you cross this bridge you will know that you have gone too far). The landscapes are park-like so long as we are beside the Moffat Water, which we soon cross by an old stone bridge and turn right in a major road to another grand ride, at first under hanging woods and then between the summits of the Tweedsmuir peaks and Ettrick Forest. The ensuing pass takes us between these two great hill massifs. It is as splendid a hill road as any in Britain. The famous Grey Mare's Tail, a spectacular waterfall, is on our left. From the point where the cascade reaches road-level a footpath leads in one and a quarter miles to Loch Skene, a moraine lake set high under the summits of the hills and quite a strenuous walk.

Now we climb to more than 1,100 ft and come into the upper reaches of the Yarrow, descending to St Mary's Loch after driving beside the Loch of the Lowes. 'Tibbie Shiel's' inn is just to the right, clearly visible from our road at the junction of Loch of the Lowes and St Mary's Loch. Opposite is a conspicuous seated statue of James Hogg on a tree-encircled green. Beyond, the road runs right along the shore of the loch, where for a short distance we overlap the previous route. Beyond it the Yarrow Water widens and at the 'Gordon Arms' we turn left for Peebles, or go straight on for Selkirk. Immediately beyond the 'Gordon Arms' Mount Benger Farm is on our left. This was the farm of which James Hogg was tenant from 1821–1830, though by all accounts he made no great success of his tenancy. It is, in fact, a rather bleak and lonely sheep farm now more spick and span and looking at its best. (The farm at which he died is about half a mile along B709 towards Ettrick and is now called Eldinhope.)

The rest is simple. We pass the little village of Yarrow, its church, just to the left of the road, built in 1635 to supersede the ruined church of St Mary by the loch. We cross the Yarrow after passing the entrance to Broadmeadows, and see on the right the fine Newark Castle, the magnificent ruin of a house which was a royal hunting lodge in the fifteenth century. Gradually the valley broadens as the Ettrick joins the Yarrow and we can see Selkirk on its hill ahead of us, with a specially fine view of the town as we bear right at river-level and climb towards it.

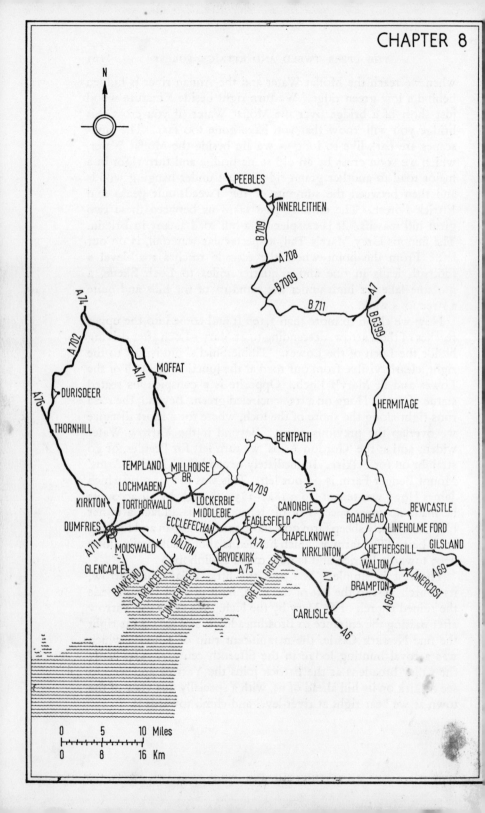

N

PEEBLES

INNERLEITHEN

B 709

A 708

B 7009

B 711

A 7

B 6399

A 74

A 702

MOFFAT

A 74

DURISDEER

A 76

THORNHILL

HERMITAGE

BENTPATH

TEMPLAND   MILLHOUSE BR.

LOCHMABEN

A 709

KIRKTON   TORTHORWALD

LOCKERBIE

MIDDLEBIE

CANONBIE

BEWCASTLE

DUMFRIES

ECCLEFECHAN

EAGLESFIELD

ROADHEAD

LINEHOLME FORD

A 711

MOUSWALD

DALTON

A 74

CHAPELKNOWE

KIRKLINTON

HETHERSGILL

GILSLAND

GLENCAPLE

BANKEND

BRYDEKIRK

A 75

WALTON

KLANERCOST

A 69

CLARENCEFIELD

GRETNA GREEN

A 7

BRAMPTON

A 69

CUMMERTREES

CARLISLE

A 6

0   5   10 Miles

0   8   16 Km

CHAPTER EIGHT

THE WESTERN BORDERLAND

FOR REASONS which are rather obscure but almost certainly include the vast popularity of the Lake District, the western borderland between England and Scotland is far less well known than the eastern. Yet there is an infinity of interest near where the counties of Cumberland and Dumfriesshire join and great beauty in the roads which closely follow the shores of the Solway Firth and climb up into the border hills on either side of Annandale. A selection of routes on the Cumberland side of the border is given in the volume in this series devoted to the Lake District and the majority of tours outlined in this chapter are, therefore, on the Scottish side, although they cross the border to places of very great interest, such as Bewcastle and Lanercost.

There are many good centres from which the whole of this countryside can be covered. Carlisle is probably the best, with accommodation to suit every purse, but Dumfries is a very good second, even though it lies on the very edge of the most Scottish part of Scotland. There is also ample accommodation along A74, the Carlisle-Glasgow road, for instance, at Lockerbie and Ecclefechan, both good centres. And, of course, there is always Gretna Green for anyone who has struggled as far as Scotland and has to wait there a fortnight!

The tour which follows is from the Tweed valley and the Scott country to the borderland near Carlisle. It is an ideal link road, included partly because many people divide their holidays between the Scott country and the western borderland, but also as a practical tour from Peebles or Selkirk, or for that matter in the reverse direction from Carlisle or Brampton. The actual distance from Peebles to Longtown is about 90 miles, so that the return journey is long for a day's tour, but quite practicable if main roads, which in this part of the country are remarkably quiet, are followed one way or the other.

If we are starting from the Scott country we make first for the

103

'Gordon Arms' on A708 by the route described in the previous chapter, or from Peebles by way of Innerleithen, following either the north or the south bank of the Tweed between the two. In either case we take B709 from the 'Gordon Arms', signposted Hawick, crossing the Yarrow Water. We reach a height of more than 1,100 ft before descending to the valley of the Tushielaw burn, which leads us to the 'Tushielaw' inn on the Hawick road. There is a glimpse of the Ettrick Water before we turn left at the inn and cross the river on the Hawick road, soon climbing high above it, again to a height of more than 1,000 ft as we approach the moorland plateau, which continues unbroken for many miles until we reach the placid Clearburn Loch on our left. Even after that there is only the occasional farmhouse at long intervals, sheep farms of no great wealth, though here and there experimental forestry is under way and it is interesting to see how the tiny trees are struggling for survival in such inhospitable surroundings.

Two or three miles further, we pass close to the Alemoor Loch, now a reservoir for the Roxburgh County Council, a fine sheet of water which enlivens the landscape on both sides of our road. Then we begin to descend, with a fine view over the valley of the Borthwick Water, and at the next two junctions prefer the Hawick turns (left and right), passing the mid-seventeenth-century church of Roberton. Finally we cross the Borthwick Water and reach A7. This sounds a rather terrifying road. Indeed it is the main road from Carlisle towards the Scott country and Edinburgh, but it is after the fashion of old-style main roads rather than the improved variety like the A74. Seldom is the traffic along it considerable. We turn right in it for Carlisle, passing the ruined keep of Goldielands high on an eminence just to the left of the road.

Now we are descending the upper Teviot valley towards Teviothead, where our road veers left away from the Teviot valley, once more into wilder country, very impressive and often attractive. At the 'Mosspaul' inn we reach the summit of the pass and the boundary between Dumfriesshire and Roxburghshire. Thence we descend the narrow gorge of the Mosspaul burn, turning left for Hermitage Castle along another beautiful valley where the summits of the hills are more rounded and the slopes comparatively gentle, with the course of the burn marked by trees, which gives a special beauty to this part of the tour.

The central square and seventeenth-century market cross, Melrose.   (Chapter 6.)

The Leithen Water above Innerleithen.   (Chapter 7.)

Farms beside the Newhall burn, and Duchar Law (1,779 ft).   (Chapter 7.)

St Mary's Loch and the surrounding green hills.   (Chapter 7.)

Beyond the summit of the pass we descend towards Hermitage and pass the castle on our left (see page 47), following the course of the Hermitage Water until we reach B6399, in which we turn right for Newcastleton. For a time the Hermitage Water keeps us company, but later joins the Liddel Water, which is with us all the way to Newcastleton as the valley gradually widens, the well-known Liddesdale, rich and fertile compared with most of the hill valleys. Newcastleton itself is a long straggling village or small town with many one-storeyed houses and a succession of trim greens shaded by trees.

At its end we bear left for Brampton, crossing the Liddel Water and bearing right again for Brampton, seeing after about two miles the well-marked entrenchments on a hill to our left, where there is an enclosed hut group on the summit. Then we bear left again for Brampton and see before us the dark mass of the Kershope Border Forest Park extending over many square miles. Crossing the Kershope burn we drive into its thickets and at the first signposted junction bear left for Roadhead by the 'Dog and Gun' inn.

When we emerge from the forest we are looking across an almost level landscape towards the Solway Firth. Bearing right at a farm we pass a church on our left before crossing the Black Lyne and at the next junction, at the top of a hill, turn right, still following the signposts for Roadhead. Then at a major road, B6318, we go forward for Gilsland, soon passing a turning to Bewcastle church, a well worthwhile detour, not only to see the church built within the confines of a Roman fort but to appreciate the artistic magnificence of one of the finest Celtic crosses in Britain, still standing in the churchyard. Going forward we bear left just beyond Roadhead post office towards Gilsland and continue to Lyneholmeford, where we cross the White Lyne and continue for Carlisle, but turn right at a subsequent T-junction, still following the road to Carlisle, which is almost like Rome in the number of roads that lead to it. We insist, however, on being nonconformist and on reaching a T-junction after nearly three miles turn right, leaving the Carlisle road, for Shankhill, but turn left a quarter of a mile further for Kirklinton, passing the handsome park and hall, which is now a hotel. Then at the church we go forward for Longtown (and again Carlisle!) but on reaching A6071 we turn firmly away from Carlisle for Longtown over the quiet pastoral landscapes of the Esk valley and on reaching A7 turn right for an easy and swift return to our various starting points via Langholm, an attractive town on the Esk.

The next tour, a particularly exciting one, is mainly in Dumfriesshire, the south-western border county of Scotland *par excellence*, crossing the English border for a visit to Carlisle, equally the western border town *par excellence*. It also contrives to include a number of historic places and a stretch of the Roman Wall in Cumberland which vies with any of the better-known parts of it further east. There is a famous priory, an equally famous castle, and a still more famous Celtic cross, all right beside the route.

The majority of motorists will find, if time permits, that it is far more manageable in the compass of two days' motoring than in one, especially as its total length, mostly on byways, amounts to 125 miles. Fortunately it can be split almost anywhere and because its shape is oval, or very nearly circular, the return journey after the first day's motoring will be a short one along main roads or semi-main roads, remembering that the main roads of south-west Scotland, apart from the influence of the Glasgow highway, are quiet country ways compared with the majority of main roads in England. That is especially true of A75, the road which links Carlisle with Dumfries, a road which is straight and wide enough to carry a much heavier flow of traffic than it is ever called upon to bear.

Dumfries itself is a town of many parts. With one eye it looks westward into the supremely Scottish landscapes of Galloway, with the other to the Solway Firth, the Lake District mountains, and the countryside which is traditionally that of the western border legends. It is a good place at which to stay (as also is Carlisle) with a number of hotels and boarding houses, good shopping within a compact area, and an entrancing walk by the banks of Nith—'Maggie by the banks o' Nith, a dame with pride eneuch', as Rabbie Burns described it. Indeed, so great is the respect in which Robert Burns is held by Scottish people that one might almost think that Dumfries was consecrated to his memory. Certainly a brief exploration of the town is an absolute must before we start on the tour.

A good starting place is the High Street, in which several of the hotels are situated and the Mid Steeple, an early-eighteenth-

century town hall (1707), is a graceful building which has now
been converted into shops. The Mid Steeple is situated in the
roadway and gives a good impression on its inner side of the
width of the roads in the Dumfries of 150 years ago. The handsome statue of Burns outside the Church of Scotland is visible
from here and almost everything you want to see you will find
within ten minutes' walk of this point. The new town hall in a
classical style is in Buccleugh Street on the way to the Nith,
where the river is crossed by a number of bridges, including the
graceful many-arched structure, the 'New Bridge' of 1792, which
is close beside the town weir and still used as a footbridge. If we
walk along the riverside we pass an attractive suspension bridge,
built in 1876, and soon reach St Michael's church, a classical
building of the eighteenth century where Burns worshipped. His
mausoleum, a domed structure on Ionic pillars erected in 1815, is
in the churchyard, its most conspicuous feature a lifesize statue of
Burns at the plough and the Muse of Poetry. Members of his
family, including his wife and son, are buried in the same tomb.
The house in which he died in 1796 is a mere stone's throw away.
So much care has been taken to preserve the memory of Dumfries
in Burns's day that the house, which is generally open to the
public, is fronted by a short stretch of the original paving stones
of the street, presenting a minor hazard to modern traffic but
offering solace, one assumes, to the true Burns lover. The Burns
relics in the house are of exceptional interest.

You may find many other things in Dumfries of interest but
those are the chief, while the banks of the Nith and St Michael's
church show the way for the opening miles of our first tour,
which starts on the Glencaple road, B725, coming remarkably
soon to open country with many a fine view over the Nith and
downstream towards Criffel, the dominant feature of every landscape in this part of the country, rising high above its lesser
fellows to a height of 1,866 ft, which looks much more than it is
because the base of the mountain is precisely at sea-level.

Glencaple is a pleasant riverside resort, gay with whitewashed cottages, beyond which we continue alongside the
broadening estuary, well known for its swift-flowing tides and
quicksands (so bathers beware), gradually bearing away from the
river into quiet pastoral landscapes, and reach a signpost for
Caerlaverock Castle, our next objective. The castle lies at the

end of a rough road to the right of our way and is an intensely interesting triangular plan castle which once belonged to the Maxwell family, later Earls of Nithsdale. Besieged by Edward I in 1300, it was partly destroyed, but raised again as one of the chief border castles and became as much palace as castle, its latest buildings dating from 1638. After seeing it we resume our road, now looking across the Solway Firth to the Lake District mountains.

We continue straight along the road as far as Bankend village and there turn right at a junction by a telephone box for Ruthwell, crossing the Lochar Water by a mellow stone bridge. Though we are still very near the firth and at one point come within little more than 100 yards of high-water mark, it is usually a silver streak away to our right. For compensation there are many long views to the hills far and near, and the landscape is pleasantly varied with belts of forestry. At the next main road junction we bear left on B725 for Clarencefield (this is really a matter of continuing along the direction of the B road we have been following) but at the next crossroads we leave it, going forward into a narrow lane which soon brings us to the church within which there is one of Christendom's most priceless treasures, the famous Ruthwell Cross, an 18-ft cross of the seventh century, wonderfully sculptured with figures and scrolls, birds and beasts, and inscribed with a poem in Runic characters. There is nothing quite like the Ruthwell Cross and it is certainly worthwhile collecting the keys at Glebe Cottage. Inside the church it is possible to have a close-up view of this wonderful link with early Christianity and observe its beauty in really good light.

Having returned the keys, we go back to the church and continue in our previous direction, bearing right after a railway bridge, neglecting a right turn, then later a left turn, as we go through a clachan (hamlet), later turning left by the wooded fringe of a park and following the estate boundary to the main road, A75. We turn right in the highroad briefly for Annan through a plantation where rhododendrons line the edge of the road and on emerging in open country take the second turning on the left, signposted Brydekirk and Eaglesfield, crossing two subsequent crossroads, both of them B roads, and soon coming to Brydekirk, a village of single-storey cottages situated on the river Annan, which we cross at the far end of the village, still making for Eaglesfield. Then at the next crossroads, short of the arterial road at Kirtlebridge, we turn right towards Annan but left at the next junction for Kirtlebridge, then right 200 yards further opposite a farm. The last stage in this elaborate manoeuvre, made necessary by the rather unpredictable operations of road builders and traffic controllers, is to turn left after one and a quarter miles into an obscure lane just before the lodge of a park, and after going under a railway bridge we finally reach the main road.

Our way is to the left, that is, towards Ecclefechan, but our purpose in coming this way is to see the Merkland Cross, a wonderfully preserved floriated cross of the fifteenth century which is in a field on the other side of the dual carriageway. As this is not, as yet at any rate, a motorway we can cross the main road on foot, leaving the car by the millhouse, where our lane joins the road, and reach the cross by a stile a few yards beyond it. The floriation is certainly worth seeing, if only for its perfection and the way in which it has resisted the elements over 500 years.

Our next objective is Eaglesfield, reached by a turning on the right in one and a half miles. At a fork near its end we bear right for Chapelknowe but in the midst of the ensuing woodlands turn sharp left for Gair. After a further stretch of woodlands, in which silver birches predominate, we bear right again for Chapelknowe and continue towards it, bearing left on reaching B6357, driving through it and after that making for Canonbie along this attractive mini-highway (it is really a quiet lane).

Canonbie is on the Esk, reached by a steep double hairpin bend, a picturesque riverside village. We bear left downhill to cross the river and on the further side of the bridge go straight on for Newcastleton, rather unexpectedly on B6357. At a crossroads we turn right on B6318 for Penton and descend to the wooded valley of the Liddel Water, which here forms the boundary between England and Scotland. We neglect the Longtown turn on our right but take the next turning on the right at a crossroads where the signpost reads Easton, and in a short half mile turn left up a narrow unsignposted hedged lane. This leads on through farmlands and over gated fields, with many a grand view retrospectively to the lowland hills and forward to the Pennines and the Lake District mountains.

Signposts are few and far between but the way is relatively easy to follow. At the first T-junction we turn left, then right almost immediately for Hethersgill, continuing to the latter along this outstandingly beautiful road, crossing one crossroads and neglecting all subsequent side turnings. Before we reach Hethersgill we join a wider road and in the village turn left at the central crossroads for Walton, continuing for Walton wherever the signposts encourage us, and otherwise going straight along this quiet byway for several miles.

Walton means 'town on the wall', a sign that here we are in the vicinity of Hadrian's Wall. We bear left into the village and by the church and green go forward then fork left at the 'Black Bull', where the signpost actually reads Hadrian's Wall and Lanercost Priory. A small, recently excavated, section of the Wall is clearly indicated on our left. We turn right for Lanercost at the next T-junction and soon come to the handsome rather than spectacular ruin of this medieval priory, of which part of the church is now used as the parish church and which is always open to the public. We leave it on our right and join a wider road for Gilsland, later keeping right for Birdoswald, passing the Banks post office, near which the vallum and ditch are clearly visible on our left beside the road, and the Banks East Turret is reconstructed on our right. A mile further we pass the Leahill Turret and yet another turret, all partially reconstructed, followed by quite a long stretch of the Wall partly built up on the right of the road. The fort of Camboglanna at Birdoswald is one of the most interesting in the whole length of the Wall and can be seen on application to the farm on whose land it stands. Just beyond the farm the wholly reconstructed walls of the fort which veer away from the road are exceptionally fine. Altogether this part of Hadrian's masterpiece is almost as impressive as that between Housesteads and Winshields Crag.

At the next T-junction we bear right for Gilsland, and right again for it at the major road T-junction, then right for Brampton. Here at Gilsland there is yet another group of Wall fragments, one only a few yards from the road in Gilsland vicarage garden (approached by a footpath), another nearly opposite stretching away in an apparently unbroken line and reaching as far as the river where one can see Willowford Bridge Abutment. That is all we shall see of the Wall but it has been well worth seeing.

We continue on the same road, going forward for Low Row at
the next junction, crossing the level crossing and turning right
for Brampton on reaching A69, continuing along this and passing
the road entrance which leads past Naworth Castle (not generally
open to the public). And so into Brampton, bearing left into the
central square past Prince Charlie's House and the attractive
market hall with clock tower above, then down the broad main
street by the large Victorian church back to the main road
towards Carlisle, forking right on B6264, the pleasantest approach
to Carlisle.

On reaching the main road just outside Carlisle to the north of
the Eden Bridge we have a choice of ways. The way into the
city is, of course, to the left over the river, which would be the
ending of our tour if we started at Carlisle. It is also the way to
take if our base is Dumfries or some other point north and we
are going to explore, however briefly, this splendid and famous
city. In that case the best place to make for is the castle and the
large car park just beyond it. So we can see the castle, one of the
finest in the north country, and reach the cathedral, an absolute
gem of medieval architecture, in three or four minutes' walk,
with the market place dominated by its elegant classical town
hall a few minutes beyond. There are many old houses (and
many handsome modern ones too), many historic corners, but
this route on foot from the castle and the cathedral to the central
square is the key to them all.

We then leave Carlisle by the main road north, crossing the
Eden and continuing to the junction with A74, where we fork
left for Gretna. An alternative byway route is to turn left at the
first traffic lights after the Eden Bridge into Etterby Street and
then continue by Rockcliffe on the Eden back to A74 and left into
Gretna Green. In either case we cross the Esk, entering Scotland
and immediately passing the first of the several 'marriage houses'.
Our direct way is by A75 for Annan but it is well worth making
the complete round of Gretna Green to see the several marriage
houses, forges, souvenir shops etc., which makes this one of the
most visited places in all Scotland, even though it is singularly
lacking in beauty, or indeed in interest other than of the legendary
blacksmith at his forge where marriages by declaration were
performed in large numbers as long as they were legal.

Continuing on A75, a broad country highway, we cross the

Kirtle Water into Rigg and pass through the pleasant royal burgh
of Annan, sparing a moment to admire its handsome classical
church and striking war memorial in the square, sparing a moment
even for its towered town hall, imposing and quite typical of
southern Scotland.   Just beyond the town we cross the river
Annan and fork left on B724 for Cummertrees, thence following
the signposts for Dumfries.   Once more the scenery is lovely on
every hand, dominated on our left by the rounded outline of
Criffel, a wonderfully pleasant change after the level landscapes
between Carlisle and Gretna.

The next tour is a much shorter one, 85 miles in all, linking
Nithsdale with the border.   As for the other tours in this chapter,
Dumfries is an excellent centre, but Thornhill, Moffat and the
many small towns near the English boundary on A74 are good
alternatives, while like the previous route described, it can very
well be brought within the compass of a whole day's tour from
Carlisle, from which we only have to drive into Scotland on A74
until reaching the point where the route crosses it.

If the start is at Dumfries we leave by A701, which is signposted
at times Beattock, then after about two miles turn left in Heath
Hall Road, which is signposted Auldgirth.   We bear right at the
first fork by a cottage (following the white line) and so come into
Kirkton, bearing right in it at the village green and pump just
short of the church, then at the next T-junction we turn left.   A
glance at the map will show that this is not the shortest way
from Dumfries to this point but it is a very pretty one and allows
us to escape from the outskirts of the town painlessly and
quickly as soon as we turn off for Auldgirth.

Here as we drive along we have the distant dark mass of the
Forest of Ae, backed by the Lowther Hills, encouraging us on our
way.   In a short quarter of a mile we fork right, now driving
through finely timbered country which has a park-like appearance.
We cross a crossroads by a lodge and go straight on at the next
fork by a group of one-storey cottages, still making directly
towards the dark mass of Ae and crossing a low moorland plateau
on which in the summer countless sheep graze, as well as some
hardy cattle.   Eventually we come to Ae village, which is perched
on the hillside above the Water of Ae, and at the junction go
forward for Closeburn, now driving parallel with the Water of Ae
and looking across it to the pine-clad slopes beyond.

Criffel across the river Nith, from Glencaple.   (Chapter 8.)

The old bridge over the Nith and town weir, Dumfries.   (Chapter 8.)

Bentpath village beside the river Esk. (Chapter 8.)

The junction of the Black Esk and White Esk and Castle O'er Forest.
(Chapter 8.)

This is a grand drive through the forest, one of the more mature of Scotland's modern forestry developments and more varied than most. Beyond it we emerge on the high moors and at the first junction turn sharp right for Mitchellslacks at a point where the lonely Loch Ettrick, hemmed in by the mountains, is only a quarter of a mile to the left. The way to Mitchellslacks is another forestry drive, later emerging on the moors, hundreds of acres of which are even now being planted, with the young trees making good progress. After a mile or so we pass the large and beautifully situated farm of Mitchellslacks, the first of several near the road, which soon reaches 1,000 ft above sea-level. When we breast the final summit a really magnificent panorama awaits us over a broad valley to the Galloway mountains.

As we descend, the detail of the fertile Nithsdale comes into view and at a T-junction near the floor of the valley we turn right, and left at the next junction to Thornhill station, coming to the outskirts of the town, now more a village than a town, by the old town cross. The tree-lined streets and gracious houses of Thornhill live long in the memory. We turn right along the main street and straight on for Kilmarnock, but in just over half a mile after passing a farm, Longmyre Mains, turn right into an un-signposted lane. This is another extremely pretty lane, crossing park-like country. We turn left at the first T-junction, passing under a railway arch and continuing beside a deep wooded ravine where the Lowther Hills are ahead of us and to our right, crossing a bent crossroads (if you know what I mean). We continue beside another lovely wooded gorge and at the next unsignposted crossroads turn right towards the church of Durisdeer under the hills.

Durisdeer is wholly charming, wholly picturesque, a village at the very end of civilization, belonging as much to the heather-covered hills as to the plain. The tiny village and the church are built round a small green, the church a very famous one which traces its history back to the thirteenth century, though the present church was not built until 1699. If you explore it you will be surprised to find very uncommon box-like pews and other interesting features. Above all, you will be amazed at the beauty of the 'Queensberry Marbles', a monument in the north transept with lifesize effigies of James, 2nd Duke of Queensberry and 1st Duke of Dover, and of his wife, Mary Boyle, daughter of

Lord Clifford, under a cupola supported on twisted columns, the whole monument recognized as one of the masterpieces of early eighteenth-century sculpture by Van Nost.

The road leaves Durisdeer on the left (that is, the left as we enter it) just below the church, quickly bringing us to a major road in which we turn right at the clachan of Durisdeermill. Thereafter we can continue without a thought of finding the way for several miles through the Dalveen Pass, up and over the Lowther Hills, with a high waterfall on our right and rugged outcrops breaking the smooth surface of the grassy slopes. It is one of the finest and most impressive rides in southern Scotland.

When we have crossed the watershed the best is over and we drive over lonely moors to reach A74, in which we turn right towards Carlisle for several dull miles, crossing Beattock Summit (1,028 ft), soon afterwards passing a railway bridge, then turning left where the signpost shows Moffat over the Greenhill Stairs, a steep road on the edge of the hills which looks down into the Elvan valley, of which there is so little left here except the track of the railway and the double track of the road. However, it is a lovely ride over this corner of the Tweedsmuir Hills and down by A701 into Moffat, of which the most charming prospect is from the hillside a mile or more before we enter it. When we do reach it we find a pleasant town which was formerly a spa, the Bath Buildings, dating from 1827, now rather quaintly the town hall. Opposite in the broad market street is the well-known Ram Fountain, while next to the town hall is the gracious Georgian Moffat House.

At the end of the main street we go straight on by A701 where the signpost reads Dumfries. The mighty roar of A74 will not be denied. Even this quiet road leads us inevitably to it, although we need drive along it to the left for less than a mile, when we turn left by the first turning, driving under it and then taking the turning which is signposted Lochmaben, B7020. By this way we follow the green fields of Annandale for some distance and then cross a low ridge into the valley of the Kinnel Water, a tributary of the Annan. Continuing straight ahead on this quiet road and crossing several crossroads, we turn right on reaching the village of Templand, following the signposts for Kirkmichael and crossing the next crossroads by a row of one-storey cottages, where our way is signposted Dumfries.

After that we neglect turnings to the right and left and at the next crossroads in a belt of woodlands turn left for Torthorwald and Dumfries, crossing the Water of Ae, here quite a broad river running over a shingle bank. In less than half a mile we turn sharp left for Torthorwald and right, again for Torthorwald, on the other side of an old railway bridge, going through a range of hills several of which are crowned by prehistoric camps and entrenchments. When finally we reach Torthorwald it is an easy run of about four miles into Dumfries along A709, and just after joining the major road we pass the substantial ruins of a castle which was once a Carlyle stronghold, one of the most conspicuous castle ruins in this part of Scotland and setting the final stamp of romance on a route which although it has never taken us very many miles from the beaten track has always seemed to be on the very edge of beyond.

The last tour in this book is certainly one of the most exciting and attractive and includes some miles of unmade road which is, however, perfectly navigable, the exquisite Lochmaben, and many miles of the Esk valley, including the outstandingly beautiful junction of the White and Black Esk, on which we look down from a high viewpoint. Added to all that there are a number of interesting and historic places along the tour, which is a mere 85 miles in all but has fully enough material to keep us busy and interested for a livelong summer's day.

Dumfries is as good a centre as any, better than most, but the route passes through Ecclefechan and Lockerbie, which are both on A74 and have ample accommodation for motorists, while once more Carlisle is a practical centre from which to attempt it, joining the route at Dumfries or at Ecclefechan. We leave the central square of Dumfries by A75 but follow it only briefly, for we leave this road between two churches in St Mary's Street, passing the railway station then following A709 towards Lockerbie. Our first stint is the same as the last few miles of the previous tour in reverse, to Torthorwald. Just beyond the keep of the Carlyles we turn right at a crossroads for Mouswald and just beyond the charming little classical church keep straight on where the signpost still reads Mouswald, climbing on to a shelf which looks across Nithsdale to Criffel and the Solway Firth. After a mile, just beyond a group of cottages and a farm, we turn left at an unsignposted crossroads on a road which takes us to several farms and then continues as an untarred road. It has, however, a good surface, rather like the hundreds of miles of untarred road in Ireland. There are a number of gates to be negotiated but the views into Nithsdale and later towards Lochmaben are compensation enough and the moorland plateau which lies between the two is colourful in the late summer.

Eventually we reach a tarred road after passing the first farm which looks into Annandale and descend steeply by a gradient of 1 in 7, with several of Lochmaben's lochs clearly visible immediately below us. We cross a minor crossroads then reach a major road where we turn left, passing the first of the five lochs of Lochmaben on our left (though it is mostly hidden behind a belt of woodland), then the extensive Castle Loch, the finest of the five, on our right. The ruined Lochmaben Castle is on a wooded promontory but it is a mere fragment and not easy to see from the loch-side. The loch is beside us right to the entrance to the town, where the distinctive church set high beyond the loch beckons us on to the pleasant main street, which has at its other end a classical town hall surmounted by a spired clock tower and a statue of Bruce in front of it.

Here we fork right along another agreeable street, mainly of bright-looking one-storey cottages, pass another of the small lochs, and soon fork right for Beattock, continuing along this road for about one and a quarter miles to a crossing of the river, immediately after which we bear right for Millhousebridge, where we reach the river Annan, cross it by a picturesque stone bridge, and on the other side turn right for Fishbeck, keeping right at a fork beyond 'Applegarth Town', now following the signpost to Dalton but turning right after a short quarter mile at a wood.

Now we are driving parallel with the distant ridge which lies between us and Nithsdale, then soon after crossing the Dryfe Water we bear left for Lockerbie, now only one and a half miles away. Before reaching Lockerbie we must cross the arterial road and in the town centre by the church and post office bear left for Langholm and right at the tall-towered town hall, again for Langholm, and left at the top of the street at a T-junction for Corrie. Lockerbie looks handsome and in driving through it we pass some handsome public buildings, but it has surprisingly little interest for the antiquarian.

We leave it behind us in a matter of two or three minutes, going over a low range of hills, wooded in places, towards Corrie and after crossing the highest point of the ridge bear right at a fork by a group of farms which are known collectively as Corrie Common, and after a short half mile, neglecting a right turn down School Lane, which is a cul-de-sac, turn right again at a T-junction, continuing along this gently descending road which commands fine views of the Stidriggs burn, which we later cross, then at a junction just short of A709 we turn squarely left uphill where the signpost reads Westerkirk, with the Water of Milk deep in a valley on our right, another extraordinarily lovely road. Later our road ascends on to open moorlands which we cross at a height of more than 700 ft yet giving the impression of being in the very centre of an extensive mountain range.

Keeping left at the Langholm turn, where we are in sight of Castle O'er Forest, covering the hillsides as far as we can see before we enter the forest, we look down at the junction of the Black Esk and the White Esk, surely one of the loveliest places in the whole of the border country, and after crossing a bridge bear right into the forest beside the White Esk, which for miles keeps us company in a wide gorge on our right. Continuing to a major road, we turn right on B709 for Langholm (at this point we are very near the route from Peebles which brought us to Eskdalemuir), following the other side of the valley of the White Esk as we make determinedly for Langholm.

Soon we leave the river valley, cross the moors, and reach the river again when its waters have been swollen by the Black Esk and the two are known collectively as the Esk. Eventually we cross the Esk, turning left for Langholm on the other side of the bridge, and passing only one village on our way to Langholm, and that on the other side of the river but a singularly beautiful one at a distance and a most attractive feature of the Esk landscape. Bentpath is its name. The church, with its typical pinnacled tower, stands on an eminence above the stone bridge and rows of tiny cottages fan out on each side of it. It is seen at its best late on a summer evening when the sun shines directly on the bridge and the church.

And so by riverside woods into Langholm, a favourite anglers' resort, and forward in it as for A7 as far as the bridge over the Esk, where we turn right without crossing the river and continue alongside it, turning right at a church and going forward in a major road. We enter the wooded valley of the Wauchope Water, soon crossing the river, and continuing towards Lockerbie for about seven miles. It is a fine ride which gives us our last mountain panoramas as once more we cross the high moors, lonely and unspoilt, yet rarely rising above 1,000 ft.

At a main road junction we bear left on B722 for Ecclefechan, a still pleasant road which takes us by Waterbeck and Middlebie, two compact, pretty but otherwise undistinguished hamlets, before running into Ecclefechan. Our direct way is through the town and on for Dalton on B725 but first we must explore Ecclefechan's quiet and picturesque main street, happily bypassed by the main road which roars on to Lockerbie. Above all, we must see Carlyle's house, a property of the National Trust of Scotland, by turning left in the old main street, when we shall find it on our right, a whitewashed house with a central archway. It is an interesting house in its own right. When it is open it is worth going in to see the surprisingly large collection of the writer's relics which are contained within it.

Afterwards we cross A74 near the church for Dalton, crossing the river Annan after 2 miles and skirting the wooded riverside of Hoddam Castle. And so through Dalton, the last of our attractive villages, yet another in which much of the effect is created by the number of one-storey cottages, bearing left past the spired church and continuing to A75, which we reach only a few swift miles from Dumfries. Even though this is not the most spectacular of conclusions, either to a tour or to a book, it serves well to underline the unusual beauty of the roads we have traversed earlier in the tour and the exquisite mantle which nature laid down on the rich earth in the valleys and on the relatively barren moorlands alike.

Motoring on Regional Byways Series
by Christopher Trent

*To serve as companions and guides to places of natural
beauty and historic interest along unfrequented ways*

NORTH OF LONDON

Byway motoring within a 50-mile radius of the metropolis north
of the Thames.

LAKELAND

Byway motoring in Cumberland, Westmorland and the Furness
district of Lancashire.

MIDLAND ENGLAND

Byway motoring within a 50-mile radius of Birmingham and the
Black Country.

SOUTH OF LONDON

Byway motoring in Surrey, Kent and Sussex.

WEST COUNTRY

Byway motoring in Somerset, Gloucestershire, Herefordshire,
Shropshire, Worcestershire.

BORDER COUNTRY

Byway motoring in Northumberland, Durham and the border
country of Scotland.

INDEX OF PLACES

Dalton, 118
Dalveen Pass, 114
Deadwater, 39
Deerness valley, 19
Denhill Park, 30
Derwent river, 22, 26
Derwent valley, 21, 25, 26
Devil's Beef Tub, 91, 95, 97
Devil's Water, 26
Dewar burn, 93
Dinnington, 41, 45
Dod Law, 67
Doddington, 67
Dollar Law, 96
Drumelzier, 98
Dryburgh, 92, 95
Dryburgh Abbey, 85, 86
Dryfe Water, 116
Duddo, 67
Duddo Stones, 67
Dumfries, 3, 4, 103, 106–7, 111, 112,
 115
Dunbar, 69
Duns, 72
Dunstanburgh Castle, 2, 55, 62
Durham Castle, 2, 13
Durham Cathedral, 5, 7, 13
Durham City, 3, 5, 13, 19, 20, 22, 25
Durham University, 13
Durisdeer, 113–14
Dye Water, 78

Eaglesfield, 109
Earlston, 84, 85
Easington, 5, 8
East Allen valley, 23, 26
East Denton, 30
East Lilburn, 66
East Woodburn, 46
Ebchester, 22
Ecclefechan, 103, 115, 118
Eddleston, 94
Eddleston Water, 94
Eden, vale of, 2
Eden river, 2, 111

Eden Water, 78
Edinburgh, 81, 89, 93
Edmondsley, 12
Edrom, 72
Eglingham, 66
Eildon Hills, 78, 82, 85, 86
Ellemford, 79
Elsdon, 37, 53
Elsdon burn, 37
Elvan valley, 114
Embleton, 62
Escomb church, 14–15
Esk river, 106, 109, 111, 117
Esk valley, 106, 115
Eskdalemuir observatory, 100
Etal, 67
Ettrick, 3, 4, 99–100
Ettrick Forest, 84–5, 87, 101
Ettrick Loch, 113
Ettrick Pen, 99
Ettrick Water, 87, 91, 99, 100, 101,
 104
Ettrickbridge, 99
Eyemouth, 70

Falstone, 46
Farne Islands, 61
Firth of Forth, 71, 79, 93
Flodden Field, 80
Floors Castle, 77, 81, 89
Font river, 44
Ford, 67
Ford Castle, 67
Fountainhall, 84

Gala Water, 83, 84
Gala Water valley, 83, 84
Galashiels, 92
Galloway, 3, 106
Galloway Hills, 100, 113
Garvald, 79
Gateshead, 5, 19, 23
Gibside Chapel, 25
Gilsland, 30, 110
Gladhouse reservoir, 94

Leithen Water, 92, 93
Liddel Water, 47, 105, 109
Liddesdale, 105
Lilburn stream, 66
Linburn beck, 16
Lindisfarne Priory, 74
Loch of the Lowes, 101
Lochar Water, 108
Lochmaben, 115, 116
Lochmaben Castle, 116
Lockerbie, 103, 115, 116
Longformacus, 78
Longhoughton, 62
Longtown, 103, 105
Lowick, 73
Lowther Hills, 100, 112, 113, 114
Lugate Water, 84
Lunedale, 17
Lyne river, 64
Lyneholmeford, 105

Manfield, 10
Manor Water valley, 94, 96
Marsden Bay, 7
Matfen, 34
Megget Water, 96
Mellerstain, 81, 82
Melrose, 4, 81, 85, 86, 92, 95, 98
Melrose Abbey, 85, 86
Merkland Cross, 109
Middlebie, 118
Middleton, 18
Minto, 88
Minto Hills, 87
Mitchellslacks, 113
Mitford, 44, 56
Moffat, 4, 91, 95, 112, 114
Moffat Water, 101
Moorfoot Hills, 3, 81, 82, 83, 91, 92, 93
Morpeth, 41, 56-7, 61
Morpeth Castle, 57
Mosspaul burn, 104
Mount Benger Farm, 101
Mountbenger, 96
Mountbenger burn, 96

Naworth Castle, 111
Neasham, 9-10
Neidpath Castle, 94-5
Netherton, 52
New Shotton, 8
Newark Castle, 101
Newbrough, 34
Newcastle-on-Tyne, 2, 5, 19, 23, 28, 29, 30, 35, 38, 41, 45, 55, 56, 61, 65
Newcastleton, 105
Newhall burn valley, 96
Newton burn, 58
Newton Don, 78
Newton-by-the-Sea, 62
Newtown, 86
Nisbet, 89
Nith river, 3, 106, 107
Nithsdale, 112, 113, 116
Norham, 68, 73
Norham Castle, 68
North Charlton, 66
North Shields, 7
North Tyne river, 32, 34, 35-7, 38, 45, 46, 47, 48

Oakwood, 32
Oakwood Tower, 99
Ogle, 41
Otterburn, 37, 41, 45, 46, 49, 50, 53
Otterburn Mill, 37
Ovingham, 28

Pease Bay, 71
Peebles, 4, 77, 92, 95, 98, 99, 103, 104
Peel Fell, 39, 47
Pennines, 5, 9, 10, 17, 19, 26, 27, 109
Percy Cross, 49
Peth Bank, 12
Piercebridge, 10
Polwarth, 78
Ponteland, 35, 41
Prendwick, 52
Preston, 79